Home Made
MODERN

Home Made MODERN

Smart DIY Designs for a Stylish Home

BEN UYEDA

Running Press
PHILADELPHIA · LONDON

To my mother and father—for putting tools in my hands,
ideas in my head, and love in my heart.

© 2015 by Ben Uyeda
Published by Running Press,
A Member of the Perseus Books Group

Printed in China

Books published by Running Press are available at
special discounts for bulk purchases in the United States
by corporations, institutions, and other organizations.
For more information, please contact the Special
Markets Department at the Perseus Books Group,
2300 Chestnut Street, Suite 200, Philadelphia,
PA 19103, or call (800) 810-4145, ext. 5000, or e-mail
special.markets@perseusbooks.com.

ISBN 978-0-7624-5507-2
Library of Congress Control Number: 2014943133

E-book ISBN 978-0-7624-5607-9

9 8 7 6 5 4 3 2 1
Digit on the right indicates the number of this printing

Cover designed by Jason Kayser
Interior designed by Frances J Soo Ping Chow
Edited by Jordana Tusman and Amy Azzarito
Typography: Pacifico, Archer, and Brandon Text

Running Press Book Publishers
2300 Chestnut Street
Philadelphia, PA 19103-4371

Visit us on the web!
www.runningpress.com

This book is intended only as an informative guide for those wishing to know more about making furniture.
Always follow safety instructions on power equipment and other tools. Information in this book is general
and is offered with no guarantees on the part of Running Press. The author and publisher disclaim all liability
in connection with this book.

Contents

1.
The
HomeMade
Modern
Philosophy

The best way to minimize waste is to make more projects from the things you already own.

Growing up in a home with four children and parents on a tight budget, my siblings and I quickly learned that if we wanted something, we'd have to figure out how to make it ourselves. Our bedtime stories consisted of books like *Robinson Crusoe*, *Swiss Family Robinson*, *Little House on the Prairie*, and *Tom Sawyer*. Whether they had a home in a treehouse or a raft for adventure, the heroes in these books made what they needed. So when, as a twelve-year-old, I wanted a sword, I found a book on DIY blacksmithing at the library and built my own forge on our concrete patio, using my mom's old hairdryer, drain pipes, cinder blocks, and a car's leaf spring. I actually managed to forge my own metal sword before the concrete grew so hot that the patio exploded.

And despite the explosion (or maybe *because* of the explosion—quite exciting for a twelve-year-old!), I was undeterred in my quest to use DIY as a way to get the things I wanted without spending much money. After a childhood spent making things, design was so ingrained in what I wanted to do that I went to school for architecture. My interest was always in doing more with less, so it wasn't a surprise when I started my own environmentally friendly firm, ZeroEnergy Design, and later, FreeGreen, a Web-based media company that distributes green home designs on the Internet.

And that's how I was spending my time, when, in 2013, I grabbed a beer with a furniture designer friend and listened to him complain about how impossible it was to design quality furniture at affordable prices. According to my friend, the fault was with corporations and consumers for their misplaced values. He seemed resigned to the fact that his career would consist of making high-end custom pieces for rich people in the hopes of eventually becoming famous enough to offer an affordable line of products made overseas. It was a complaint I'd heard before from many of my designer friends. Maybe it was just the beer talking, but I bet him that I could get one thousand pieces of American-made furniture into homes across the country.

I knew it was the labor costs that were putting high-end designs out of reach for the average person. So I decided to design a piece of furniture and make a YouTube video that included all the instructions, just to see if I could get a thousand people to make it. In my mind, DIY was the only logical way to create affordable, well-designed furniture.

So far, that initial project—a concrete bucket stool (see page 73)—has been made on five continents by more than five thousand people. The response was so tremendous and unexpected that I continued designing as much affordable furniture as I could, and I started a website as a way to share those easy-to-follow modern DIYs.

On the site, I've been able to prove that it's possible for sturdy furnishings made from materials like solid wood, concrete, and steel to cost even less than cheap, store-bought plastic and particleboard furniture. But it's become more than simply using DIY as a way to obtain covetable furniture (although we have plenty of that!), because when you become more conscious of the things you're bringing into your life, you can manage your financial resources *and* make an impact on the over-consumption of the planet's resources.

The collection of projects that make up this book enable you to furnish every room in your house with quality, sustainable furniture made with your own hands. Once you start making high-grade, durable furniture, you'll notice the difference between what you're able to make and the low-quality, mass-produced furniture on the market. Following the instructions I've laid out in this book, you'll be able to create furniture that's totally individualized to your personal style, taste, and lifestyle.

Why Is DIY Important?

You can have nice things . . . if you learn to make them.

If you've walked into a modern design furniture store lately, there's a good chance that you suffered from serious sticker shock. With prices running into the hundreds for a single chair, it might feel as if beautiful, modern design is only available to the select few with pockets deep enough to afford it. The low-price furniture options are usually made with inferior materials with compromises in manufacturing ethics, and there doesn't seem to be much middle ground. So what's a design-minded, budget-conscious individual to do? I'm going to show you how to roll up your sleeves and make beautiful, well-designed furniture by yourself.

For most Americans it would seem extravagant to employ a housekeeper or private chef. Why hire someone to do what can easily be done without outside help? The same pleasure that we take in keeping a clean house or cooking a healthy meal for our families can also apply to furnishing our home. In fact, think of the projects in this book as recipes. I've laid out the basic techniques and ingredients, but I urge you to run with it by changing the color, size, or material. I've also done my best to supply quantities and sizes, but keep in mind that these will vary depending on the materials you use.

One of the best parts of making your own furniture is that you can personalize each project to fit your own style and taste. As long as you understand the basic concept behind each project, you should be able to really make it your own. This is the path to more conscious consumption. It's both an opportunity to save money and acquire exactly what you want.

Setting Expectations: I'm Not a Craftsperson!

Precision is not beauty. Otherwise, all nice things would be machine-made.

The Japanese have a philosophy called *wabi-sabi*, which is in essence the art of finding beauty in imperfection. There's no direct translation in English, but the philosophy involves valuing authenticity over perfection. While most of the skills associated with woodworking and furniture involve *some* precision, the more we appreciate the asymmetrical idiosyncrasies of the handmade object, the happier we'll be with our final result.

I've seen a lot of first-time DIYers get discouraged when the piece they're working on isn't precise. I tell them that perfect precision is made in a factory, not handmade at home. Since I'm not a professional carpenter and don't have formal woodworking training, I've tried to design pieces where the inevitable flaws add to the handmade aesthetic.

Spending your weekends making furniture you love should make your life better, not add to your frustration. The only thing you need to obsess over is safety; you can relax about everything else. If you don't believe that precision can be ugly, take a stroll in the furniture aisle of the closest mega store. The edges of the furniture might be perfect, but the laminated particleboard certainly isn't. I prefer rugged materials assembled in clever ways.

These projects are purposely designed with imperfection in mind, and scuffs and scratches only enhance their handcrafted look. The concrete may crack, the wood may warp, you may need to slide a matchbook under a table leg to make it level. That's all okay! If you find yourself getting frustrated with uneven edges, warped wood, and corners that aren't at perfect 90-degree angles, remember that a world where everything is precisely 3-D printed is about as exciting as the prospect of every meal being made from powdered supplements.

Key points:

- Don't worry about anything other than safety. These projects are intended to make your life better, not more complicated.
- Precision is overrated and often ugly. There is beauty in imperfection!
- Use the projects as recipes, and feel free to deviate. This is your adventure in furniture building, so once you understand the concepts, you can use the projects as inspiration to create something that perfectly fits into your life.

What We Mean by Affordable and Sustainable

Creating a fair and sustainable society simply means trying to do a little better today than we did yesterday.

Your DIY projects won't save the world, but they can greatly reduce your impact on it, and if everything does go to hell, it will be nice to have some handy skills during the zombie apocalypse. I'm not the most militant pursuer of sustainability, but it feels good to try. Connecting even a small portion of your consumption with your responsibility to the planet is a good thing. We should at least try to make things that are a little bit better than their most common alternatives. Let's lay out some conceptual benchmarks:

Affordable + Accessible

According to the U.S. government, the average American household spends approximately $500 a year on furniture. That excludes virtually all designer brands and even puts Ikea on the limits of affordability.

The projects in this book may require a bit more dedication to assemble, but the result is a better, more affordable option than Ikea alternatives. This is not to bash Ikea, because I love some of their non-particleboard products, but I've seen too many dumpsters with barely used pieces with silly Scandinavian names poking out of them to believe that there aren't better ways to go modern on a budget.

I aimed for the projects in this book to be comparable or cheaper than their store-bought counterparts, but depending on what materials you have on hand or have access to, the furniture prices can vary. Purchasing tools might be the most expensive part of these projects, but if you make three to four DIY projects instead of buying three to four pieces of furniture, the tools will most likely pay for themselves. Because you're using your own labor, you're saving yourself the cost of the production, which means you can put some of that savings into quality materials. By doing the work yourself, you'll get furniture made with real, chemical-free wood rather than particleboard, or with solid metals rather than cheap plastic.

Recyclable + Reusable

While recycling is a much better option than simply throwing unneeded items in the garbage, an even better solution is to reuse those materials. I try to use new materials thoughtfully and sparingly. For example, I might turn a wine bottle into a drinking glass by cutting off the top and sanding down the edges. This decreases the amount of waste in the recycling bin while also creating something useful—all for the cost of a bottle of wine. Throughout this book, I'll make suggestions for ways to reuse the projects once you've grown tired of them. Remember that even recycling uses a significant amount of energy, so our goal is to reduce total energy consumption.

Durable + Degradable

The best decision we can make for the environment is to buy less stuff. But when we do buy something, we should think about the full lifecycle of that product. My goal for every DIY project is that the finished project will last indefinitely or compost quickly. There might be projects that you grow tired of, so I've provided suggestions for how to give old projects a new look or new use. For this reason, I often choose not to "protect" the wooden projects with plastic finishes, not only because I would rather feel wood when I touch it, but also because if I turn that table into something else I won't have to sand off the finish, which creates a cloud of polyurethane or acrylic dust particles that are absorbed into the soil, water, and my lungs.

Thinking about the complete lifecycle of an item can also be helpful when you're on the fence about buying something. For example, I have purchased pre-made steel table legs because I know that they'll last forever and can be removed from the table and reused for a different project.

Healthy + Whole

Our DIY projects focus on affordable, sustainable uses of natural materials such as wood, metal, and concrete. We'll use these materials both in their raw states, such as construction lumber, but for convenience, we'll also make use of readymade wood and metal products that are made without plasticized coatings. While DIYing alone won't necessarily make your home healthier, exercising the power to control the materials that come into your house certainly will. Throughout this book I've made suggestions for finishes and products that are relatively chemical-free. Not only are these better for the environment, but it also means there will be less off-gassing (the release of harmful gases trapped in some factory-made furniture and paints). And if you have a couple of rug rats who occasionally like to gnaw on the legs of the coffee table, isn't a beeswax finish preferable to a factory-applied polyurethane one?

2.
Hunting, Gathering, and Investing

Making careful decisions about the materials you use will prevent you from overspending or using anything unsafe for the environment.

Even in the middle of a city, there are opportunities to harvest the materials you need. In fact, finding the materials is often the easiest part; having space to store all your materials until you've accumulated enough to make the project might be the real challenge! For example, wood pallets are relatively easy to find but are awkward to store, and there may be rough edges and rusty nails to contend with. Opportunistic scavenging and smart shopping strategies can make your DIYs affordable, but I've learned the hard way that using a cheap or inappropriate tool can make building your own furniture a frustrating experience and can even lead to mistakes that waste materials. It's important to know where to save and when to make an investment in your DIY lifestyle.

The Materials

Once you open your eyes to the possibilities of DIYing, you'll be amazed at the amount of materials available either for the taking or at extremely affordable prices. The real challenge is in understanding the different characteristics of the materials and also finding ones compatible with the tools available to you. I often use materials for applications other than their intended purpose. For example, most woodworkers try to hide the exposed edges of plywood, while I love the stratified aesthetic. My primary concerns in choosing materials are: Is it toxic? Is it safe to work with? Do I have tools to cut it?

Wood

Wood is not a static or uniform material; it's a matrix of cells that changes with temperature and time. It warps, shrinks, changes color, and scratches easily. These are not liabilities, but organic characteristics that attract us to wood furniture. If you don't try to force wood to act like plastic or steel, it's rather easy to work with.

Construction Lumber and Softwoods

For most of my solid wood projects I use construction lumber in the form of 2×4s, 2×6s, 2×8s, 2×10s, and 2×12s. I also frequently use ¾-inch pine boards in widths ranging from 1½ inches to 12 inches.

Construction lumber is the most affordable type of large, readily available, solid wood, usually purchased by the piece instead of by the foot. Construction lumber is cheaper than finished lumber because it's not put through the same drying and stacking process. Of course, with this fiscal advantage comes some challenges. It's more likely to warp as it dries, and many of the pieces have large cracks or knots.

WHAT TO KNOW: Interestingly enough, 2×4s are not actually 2" × 4". They are actually 1½" × 3½". If you're not a math nerd, don't worry about remembering this. I'll do all the calculating for you. Just follow the diagrams and instructions. When buying wood for a particular project, keep in mind where the piece will go. If it's destined for the outdoors, you might want to spring for cedar or redwood, both of which weather well but cost a bit more than a standard 2×4. Never use pressure-treated lumber. It's extremely toxic and gross!

WHERE TO BUY: Buy construction lumber and softwoods at your local home improvement store. Find a store with a large selection to pick through to find pieces with minimal warping and knots. Just trust your eye and purchase the straightest piece that meets your aesthetic requirements. Here's a little money-saving tip: Oftentimes, you can buy long 12-foot or 16-foot pieces and have them cut down, which is usually cheaper than purchasing multiple, smaller pieces to start with. (Note: In my experience, Home Depot is the only store that will cut the wood to size without charging you. Call your local home improvement store to check on its particular policy.)

WHERE TO SCAVENGE: Construction lumber is commonly used as the structural framing for houses. Many residential construction sites are littered with cut-off ends, and the contractor is often willing to give them away.

Hardwoods

Hardwoods, like walnut or maple, are increasingly rare and expensive. I don't use them often, but when I do I try to use them efficiently and dramatically. Hardwoods are typically sold by the "board foot," which is actually a measure of volume. A board foot is 12" × 12" × 1".

WHAT TO KNOW: Imported tropical hardwoods are not always harvested ethically. Look for ones that are FSC-certified. (These are woods certified "green" by the Forest Stewardship Council.)

WHERE TO BUY: Rather than your home improvement store, make a trip to a lumberyard or a fine woodworking store.

WHERE TO SCAVENGE: Hardwood flooring can sometimes be salvaged from construction sites or purchased on Craigslist at a discounted price. To save time, set up Craigslist alerts to be notified when particular types of wood are being offered.

Logs

Log furniture isn't typically considered modern, but I like to mix in the occasional log or live-edge piece (this is the type of wood where the natural edge of the piece is visible) into an otherwise modern setting for a bit of texture.

WHAT TO KNOW: Logs can be found on the cheap, but they will most likely experience significant cracking and warping.

WHERE TO BUY: Search Craigslist for "firewood" and you're bound to find opportunities to purchase cheap logs. I have consistently found solid hardwood logs this way for just a few dollars apiece.

WHERE TO SCAVENGE: If you live near a wooded area, you can easily scavenge for fallen branches or even full trees, particularly after significant storms. I've found really nice pieces of hardwood that would have otherwise ended up as firewood or simply rotted away. If you're scrounging on public lands, make sure you check your local laws before taking fallen branches or logs home with you. Logs collected from the outdoors will warp and crack as they dry and can be difficult and cumbersome to work with, so look for the driest piece you can find. Also be sure to check for mold. If you don't see any but the log smells moldy, move on.

Composites: Plywood and Laminates

Plywood is made from thin layers of wood veneer glued and pressed together. This results in large, smooth flat boards with stratified edges. Traditionally, woodworkers would try to hide these edges, but I like the layered look and try to incorporate it into my designs.

Plywood typically comes in 4' × 8' sheets and in thicknesses ranging between ¼ inch and ¾ inch. I typically use furniture-grade or sanded plywood for my projects; it's a little more expensive but it's smoother than rougher-looking construction-grade plywood.

Laminate or melamine board is an engineered wood product with a laminated plastic coating. I use these panels to make formwork (temporary or permanent molds) for concrete. The waterproof plastic coating creates a smooth finish on concrete projects. Laminates typically come in 4' × 8' panels that are ¾ inch thick and can be quite heavy.

WHAT TO KNOW: Plywood behaves differently than solid woods. For the best results when cutting it, use a plywood blade on a circular saw.

WHERE TO BUY: I don't usually recommend specific brands, but in this case, I strongly suggest PureBond plywood, a brand that uses a formaldehyde-free technology that's healthier for your family and the environment. It promotes healthy indoor air quality due to its proprietary, soy-based adhesive (instead of potentially hazardous urea-formaldehyde).

Traditional plywood contains a lot of glues and adhesives that can off-gas formaldehyde into your home. Look for PureBond at your local home improvement store.

WHERE TO SCAVENGE: Plywood is one of those materials that I recommend you buy new. Even though you might be able to find discarded plywood, I think it's important to invest in the formaldehyde-free plywood to protect the air quality in your home.

Metal

From the time I tried to make my own sword, I've been drawn to metalworking. There's not another material that has such strength, permanence, and precision. Once you machine it, it doesn't warp or change dimensions. That durability means that the metal components used in these projects will last for quite a long time, so I always provide options to reuse them if you grow tired of the project.

Steel

Steel comes in different-shaped profiles. Angle irons and flat bars are the ones I use most often. You can drill through steel fairly easily with a normal drill, but cutting it takes some time. When I use steel, I try to get it precut to the appropriate length. If I do cut it, I use an angle grinder with a cutting blade.

WHAT TO KNOW: Raw steel is sold "dirty" because the dirt and oil helps keep the steel from rusting. To use it at home, you'll need to clean it and then protect it from rusting. Clean the steel using a non-toxic degreaser. You can protect it from rusting by applying a coat of mineral oil. If you don't want to use oil because your finished project might come in contact with your clothing, use paste wax instead.

WHERE TO BUY: Home improvement centers keep a basic selection in stock. If I need longer or unusual pieces, I will go to my local steel yard where I can order pieces by the foot.

WHERE TO SCAVENGE: While steel is every-where, it can be hard to separate it from whatever it might be attached to. However, old bed frames can be a good source for cheap angle irons.

Iron Pipe Fittings

Iron pipe fittings are like Legos for adults. They're versatile, durable, and look great when paired with wood or concrete. These ready-made pieces of iron come pre-threaded, making it easy to turn them into sturdy structures simply by twisting them together. They can be pricey, but they'll last a lifetime if cared for correctly and can always be repurposed for something new. They come in a variety of different sizes, but I typically use ½-inch, ¾-inch, and 1-inch pipes. They're available in a black or raw finish and can rust if left outside. Galvanized pipes and fittings have a protective zinc coating that prevents them from rusting as easily and gives them a light gray appearance. T fittings and flanges are two of the more common types of fittings I use.

WHAT TO KNOW: Surprisingly, ¾-inch pipes do not have a ¾-inch diameter. The ¾ inch is a nominal dimension; the actual diameter is 1.050 inches.

WHERE TO BUY: I buy mine at either my local home improvement store or plumbing supply shop.

WHERE TO SCAVENGE: You can often find sections of plumbing pipe at junkyards, but make sure the threaded ends are still in good working condition.

Metal Tubing

EMT conduit, copper, and aluminum tubing are soft metal products that are easy to work with and can be bent or cut without power tools. A simple, handheld tube cutter can quickly and precisely cut these tubes down to size. An EMT conduit (the EMT stands for electrical metallic tubing) is one of the cheapest DIY materials available, whereas copper and aluminum tubing can be quite pricey.

WHAT TO KNOW: Metal tubing has both plumbing and electrical applications, so it won't be found in a single department of a home improvement store. Look in both sections if you're having trouble finding it.

WHERE TO BUY: EMT tubing is usually available in the electrical section, where you can find it in 5- or 10-foot lengths. Copper and aluminum tubing can be ordered online or found at specialty plumbing stores.

WHERE TO SCAVENGE: Junkyards often sell metal tubing. It can be a great place to find copper or bronze tubing that already has a nice patina on it.

Concrete

Concrete is the most underappreciated DIY material. It's cheap and easy to use, but it's capable of producing long-lasting, durable pieces of furniture. An 80-pound bag can be purchased for less than $5, and you can make incredible pieces without using power tools. Concrete takes on the properties of whatever material you pour it into. If you cast it into a form made from weathered fence boards, it will have a rough, powdery texture with a visible wood grain pattern, but if you cast it into a plastic form, it will come out as smooth as glass. You can even add a pop of color to your concrete projects by painting them with a non-toxic or low-VOC paint.

Premium Concrete

I always upgrade to the premium concrete from the standard. Just a dollar more and you'll get concrete with much smaller aggregate that's also easier to work with. Quikrete 5000 is my go-to concrete mix for all sorts of DIY projects. It's stronger and cures faster than standard mixes and has a nice gray color. The only challenging thing about working with Quikrete is moving the 80-pound bags it comes in.

Specialty Concrete

For intricate casting or applications that require high-strength concrete, I order a specialty countertop mix. My favorite is Quickrete Countertop Mix, a high-performance mix that is worth the price. It doesn't have any large pieces of gravel or aggregate, which makes it great for small, intricate pieces like lamps and vases. It's also easy to work with and comes in different colors.

WHAT TO KNOW: Concrete is heavy and messy. The biggest challenges are moving it where you want it and cleaning up the mess when you're done. Also, it's hard on your skin, so I advise you to wear gloves when working with it. When mixing concrete, be sure to use clean water. Any debris in your water will ultimately show up in your project.

WHERE TO BUY: You can find standard concrete at your local home improvement store, but usually the specialty concrete isn't in stock. Just call ahead and ask to have it ordered for you.

WHERE TO SCAVENGE: It's difficult to scavenge for unmixed concrete, so unless you get lucky and find an unopened bag on Craigslist, this is an item that you'll have to purchase.

Ready-Mades

For many of these projects we use simple construction materials, but I also often appropriate ready-made wooden pieces for uses other than their original purposes: fir stair balusters, oak table legs, trim boards, and wood dowels all make regular appearances in my projects.

Ready-made metals are also a go-to resource for adding durability to a piece of furniture. Many of the pieces—from tables to benches—use metal table legs, which give an added heft to the furniture pieces.

Wood Ready-Mades

WHAT TO KNOW: Some ready-made pieces may have a plasticized or painted finish that might create toxic dust when removed. Be sure to only purchase *unfinished* items.

WHERE TO BUY: You can find many unfinished ready-mades at bigger home improvement stores like Home Depot and Lowes. Walking down the ready-made aisles of these stores is inspiring! There's so much you can do with all those pieces.

WHERE TO SCAVENGE: I'll often check out thrift stores and garage sales to see if I can find solid-wood pieces of furniture that are worth reusing.

Metal Ready-Mades

WHAT TO KNOW: Many of my projects use ready-made metal legs. Metal legs are so durable that even if the tabletop or bench top wears out, chances are you can still reuse the legs. One of my favorite styles is the hairpin leg. These metal legs, invented in 1941, were a testament to wartime efficiency—using only the minimal amount of steel to maintain the strength of a traditional leg. Their mid-century modern look is minimal and certainly ages well. After all, if we haven't grown tired of them after nearly seventy-five years, it must be a look that lasts—a classic. Another style I like is the metal trestle leg. This leg is the perfect complement to tables and desks.

WHERE TO BUY: On the HomeMade Modern Website I sell legs that are custom-made in Colorado, but you can find metal legs just about anywhere. And if for some reason you can't track a pair of hairpin legs down, the design is so simple that you can actually take a photo to any metal worker and have a set custom-made. You can also find the trestle table legs at Ikea.

WHERE TO SCAVENGE: While you might be able to find used legs on Craigslist or eBay, this is most likely going to be a material where you'll need to invest. Keep your eyes open though, because you might get lucky and find a discarded piece of furniture that allows you to easily remove the legs.

The Tools

Tools can definitely be an investment, but when you compare the price of new furniture to the cost of a piece you've made yourself, even if you include the price of new tools you'll still come out ahead. Rather than buying every tool on this list, I suggest building your tool collection around specific projects as needed. A great place to start is a cordless drill—nearly every project in this book uses one. The projects are designed around standard tools, not specialty tools that you'll only need for one job. Many of us don't have the luxury of a garage or extra storage space. We need our tools to be workhorses in our lives. And if you don't have the perfect tool for the job, try changing the job to fit the tools you *do* have!

Hand Tools

The hand tools I use most often are cheap, durable, and readily available.

KNIFE: A knife or box cutter is the hand tool I use most often. A good one features a comfortable handle with replaceable razor blades that fit in the tip. I use my knife to round the edges of 2×4s, to scrape adhesive labels off pipe fittings, and to cut away dried glue from concrete formwork.

HAMMER: I prefer fastening materials together with screws as opposed to nails, but a hammer is still a handy thing to have around. I also use it with a chisel for shaping wood.

CHISEL: This primitive tool still comes in handy for making recesses in wood. It comes in a variety of shapes and sizes, but one narrow and one wide chisel are all you should need.

HANDSAW: I rarely cut anything large with a handsaw, but if you haven't added a power saw to your collection yet there are some viable alternatives. In particular, Japanese handsaws are extremely useful for small and medium-size projects and can achieve incredibly exact cuts. I use my Japanese handsaw for trimming dowels and making small, precise cuts.

CLAMPS: Clamps are like having a second set of hands. They make everything else you do safer and more accurate. Two small C-clamps and two medium bar clamps are all you should need in your workshop.

PLIERS: I regularly use three different types of pliers: long-nose or needle-nose pliers for grabbing things in tight places, diagonal pliers for cutting wire or clipping zip ties, and locking pliers (brand name Vise-Grip) for gripping stubborn bolts or pipe fittings.

Power Tools

These are the basic power tools I use for most of my projects. When you're ready for an upgrade, the heavy-duty bench-top power tools will make large projects easier.

Portable Power Tools

CORDLESS DRILL: This is the single most useful tool I own. From obvious functions like drilling holes and driving screws to less common applications such as stripping paint and grinding metal, an 18-volt drill provides power and versatility. I've had great results with my Ryobi 18-volt drill, which features an LED light that's great for working in dark spaces.

ORBITAL SANDER: You don't necessarily *need* an orbital sander, but it sure makes the job go a lot faster. It's also one of the least expensive power tools I own. The sandpaper discs "Velcro" right to the machine, making changing out the paper fast and easy. I keep 50-, 80-, 120-, and 220-grit sanding discs on hand. If you don't

have an orbital sander, you can also sand your projects by hand.

CIRCULAR SAW: A circular saw is good for making straight cuts. It will easily cut 2×12s down to size or rip an entire sheet of plywood in half. The key to using a circular saw effectively is learning to make precise right-angle cuts. A speed square is a helpful tool for this, as it keeps crosscuts at a right angle. For long cuts through plywood and other sheet goods, clamp down a straight piece of wood first to guide the circular saw.

JIGSAW: I use a jigsaw for making curved cuts. If you don't have a circular saw you can use a jigsaw in a pinch to make straight cuts, but it isn't nearly as precise. This tool is less intimidating than a circular saw and some novice DIYers feel more comfortable using a jigsaw despite its difficulties when making precise straight cuts through thick pieces of wood.

CHAINSAW: Chainsaws are intimidating at first and definitely should be handled with care. I use mine for shaping log furniture and harvesting fallen trees and branches into usable wood. I prefer electric chainsaws to gas. They make less noise and less mess.

MULTI TOOL: A multi tool is a small handheld power tool that comes with different attachments that can be used for cutting or sanding drywall, metal, wood, plastic, composite, and many other materials. It uses a vibrating motion instead of a spinning blade and is great for cutting in tight spaces.

Bench-Top Power Tools

COMPOUND MITER SAW: A miter saw is like a circular saw except that it's attached to a base, making precise cutting extremely easy. You don't need one, but you might want one. The blade can also be adjusted to make angled cuts, making mitered corners equally simple to accomplish.

ANGLE GRINDER: An angle grinder is a powerful tool that is useful for cutting metal or roughly sanding wood. I use my angle grinder for quickly shaping log furniture.

DRILL PRESS: A drill press can make perfectly perpendicular holes in any material you're drilling, including metal. Although you can drill holes through steel using a handheld portable drill too, it's a much easier task with a drill press.

TABLE SAW: A table saw is used to make long, precise straight cuts. I use it as a more accurate alternative to a handheld circular saw when I'm cutting through multiple sheets of plywood.

Hardware and Connectors

The primary challenge in building is deciding exactly how to connect the different components together. In our modern society where cheap manufacturing is king, most furniture is glued together using high-strength, and usually high-toxicity, glues. It's a shame because the intricate details of how you join materials are a hallmark of quality craftsmanship. For our projects we're going to use connectors like screws and nails that can easily be removed so that the entire piece can be disassembled and reused.

SCREWS: Screws are the most common connectors I use. The threads of a screw are designed differently for different materials.

For most applications I use exterior deck screws. They are strong and have a protective coating that prevents rust. Occasionally, I'll spend extra money on stainless steel screws for aesthetic reasons. Screws are a structural upgrade over nails and can be used in combination with glue for super-strong wood-to-wood connections. And while I've given you screw sizes for all the projects, you'll save money if you buy a large box of deck screws and use them for all the projects. How many screws you use for each project will vary. You want the connection to be strong without overdoing it.

NAILS: I use nails when I want a clean wrought-iron head to show or when it's faster and a stronger connector isn't necessary. Finishing nails, with their small heads, can be used to connect wood while having a minimal aesthetic impact.

BRACKETS: Brackets are metal braces with pre-drilled holes to attach them. They're useful for quickly increasing the strength of a structure and are available in a variety of different sizes and finishes.

GLUES: Glue is an easy but often messy way of connecting materials. I use a hot glue gun for temporary applications like making concrete formwork. I use wood glues in combination with screws for strong wood connections. Occasionally, I use high-strength epoxies for connecting different types of materials together, like metal and plastic, but only if I can't figure out a different option, because they tend to have toxic properties and can be expensive.

ZIP TIES: Zip ties, also known as tie wraps and cable ties, are useful connection devices for both temporary applications (see Herb Garden Wall, page 118) and permanent applications (see Zipstitch Chair, page 90). I use them to secure materials I want to store away and as flexible connectors between pieces of wood in some projects.

BOOK CODES

BISCUIT

BELT SANDER

BUCKET

C-CLAMP

CHISEL

CIRCULAR SAW

CONCRETE (BAG)

CONCRETE (LOOSE)

COMPOUND MITER SAW

DIAGONAL PLIERS/ WIRE CUTTERS

DRILL PRESS

DRILL BITS

DRILL

DRUM SANDER

GLUE

GLUE GUN

HAIRPIN LEG (TABLE)

HAMMER

HEX NUT

HAIRPIN LEG (BENCH)

HINGE

HOE

HOLE SAW

IRON PIPES

JIGSAW

KNIFE/ BOX CUTTER

KNITTING NEEDLES

L-BRACKET

LEGO®

LEVEL

LONG-NOSE PLIERS

MIXING BOWL

MIXING SPOON

MULTI-TOOL

NAIL

ORBITAL SANDER

PAINT

PAINTBRUSH (BRISTLE)

PENCIL

PLASTIC MIXING BIN/TUB

PRY BAR

RAG

RULER

RECIPROCATING SAW

50-GRIT SANDPAPER

80-GRIT SANDPAPER

120-GRIT SANDPAPER

220-GRIT SANDPAPER

SCREW

SHOVEL

SQUARE

TAPE MEASURE

TROWEL

TUBE CUTTER

WATER

WIRE BRUSH

ZIP TIE

CUT AT HOME DEPOT

3-D PRINTER

3.
The
Projects

LIVING ROOM

Plywood Media Console

Gone are the days of the giant, oversized media center cabinet. Televisions have slimmed down dramatically and even AV components are smaller. This entire console is made from strips of plywood stacked and screwed together, which makes it easily customizable. Simply cut and arrange the strips of plywood to create different sized openings that will neatly store all your randomly sized media components.

Estimated Time:

3 to 6 hours

Estimated Cost:

Under $50 without legs
  ($100 with legs added)

Supplies:

1 to **2** 4' × 8' sheets of ¾"-thick furniture-
  grade plywood with a sanded finish
1¼" wood screws
2 concrete blocks (optional)
4 hairpin legs (optional)
¾" screws (optional)
Low-VOC latex paint (optional)

Tools:

Pencil
Ruler
Circular saw
220-grit sandpaper
Clamp (optional)
Straightedge
Cordless drill with driving bit
Paintbrush (optional)

NOTE: You can mix and match plywood
if you want different stripe patterns in
the laminations.

1: Plan your layout and mark out the cuts

Determine the overall size of the console you want. Then determine how many openings you want and the size of each. (See the diagram opposite.) Once you have established your layout, use a pencil and a ruler to mark out the cuts.

2: Cut the plywood into strips

Cut the plywood along the marked lines using the circular saw. (See the diagram for cuts and sizes.) My saw has a laser guide that makes creating straight cuts easier. If you don't have a laser guide and want super-precise cuts, clamp a straightedge to the plywood to guide the circular saw. Use 220-grit sandpaper on the edges of the plywood to remove splinters and tear-out that may have resulted from the saw.

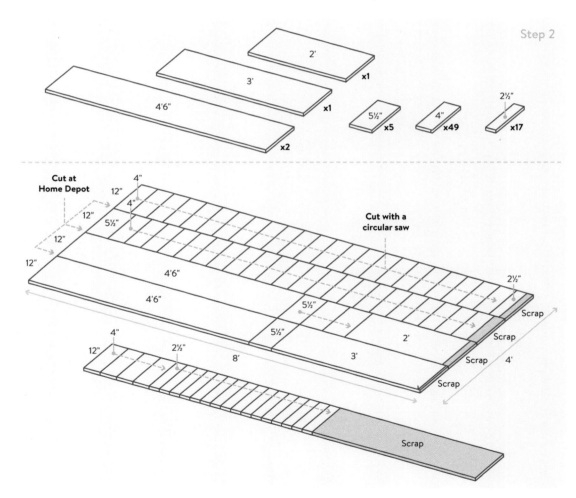

Step 2

2' x1
3' x1
4'6" x2
5½" x5
4" x49
2½" x17

Cut at Home Depot
Cut with a circular saw

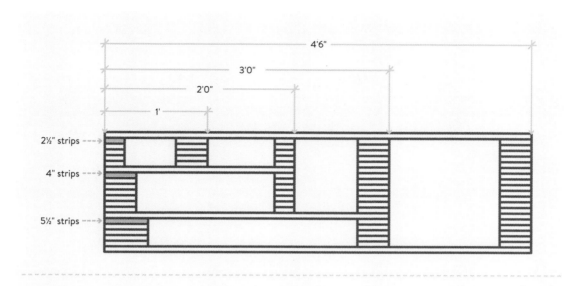

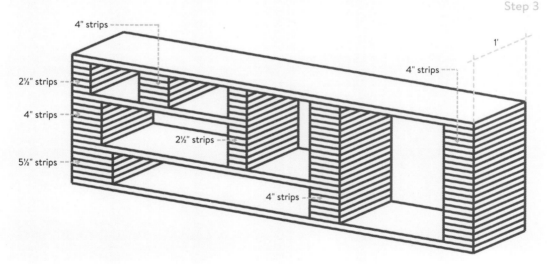

Step 3

3: Assemble the console

Lay the top piece upside down. Position the pieces for your first layer on top and secure them with screws using the cordless drill. Assemble the console top to bottom so that the screws don't show through the top piece of plywood. Two screws are usually enough to hold the smaller strips (in my case, 2½" wide), but three screws are better for anything wider. Attach one layer at a time to slowly build them up. Finish with the bottom piece of plywood, then turn the console right side up.

4: **Add legs!**

While this console works perfectly flat on the ground or up on a pair of concrete blocks, I like to add some premade hairpin legs for a more finished look. Screw through the holes in the hairpin legs with ¾" screws to fasten the legs to the bottom of the plywood console.

Optional

5: **Add a painted plywood back**

Use a scrap ¼"-thick piece of plywood to make a back for the console. Paint it before securing it with screws to add a nice contrast to the layered plywood.

What can go wrong?

You didn't buy enough plywood.

Carefully plan out the console beforehand to ensure that you buy the right amount. That being said, it's a good idea to always budget 10 to 20 percent extra. This will make up for any mistakes, last-minute design changes, and the small amount that gets turned into sawdust from the numerous cuts.

Your cuts are crooked.

If your cuts are crooked or not perfect right angles, your console will have a rougher texture.

The stacked pieces might look more like a messy pile of papers than perfectly organized books. It's not necessarily a bad thing, and some people even prefer this look. In fact, the rough, layered texture is the reason many people like this project.

There are gaps between the plywood layers.

Gaps can occur when the screw pushes up the top layer of wood when securing it. To prevent this, firmly hold the plywood down against the layer below while screwing.

Alternatives

Use this same stacking technique to make larger or smaller versions of this console. The taller you make your console, the more important it is to minimize gaps between the layers when screwing them together. If you have a table saw, you can make a very precise version of this project. You can also experiment with different types of plywood or even eco-friendly particleboard, or oriented strand board. Painted MDF can be an attractive alternative as well.

What if you don't want it anymore?

The nice thing about screwing the layers together instead of gluing them is that you can always unscrew and rearrange them to create different sized compartments and shelves. If you get tired of the console altogether, use the plywood pieces to make handy little storage boxes.

Iron and Wood Console

If you want your high-tech, modern-looking flat screen juxtaposed with something a little more rustic and industrial, this is the media console for you. Typically, projects with multiple materials and dynamic non-orthogonal angles are difficult, but luckily this isn't one of those. This project uses geometry and gravity to hold itself up on a sturdy set of iron legs made from plumbing pipe. Pipe furniture tends to all look the same, but this project uses pipes at an angle to create a unique look. You can make this project at any length you like, but I used a single 12-foot-long 2×12 so that the finished size is a little more than 5 feet long.

Estimated Time:
3 hours

Estimated Cost:
Under $75

Supplies:
1 12'-long 2×12
2½" deck screws
Linseed oil
¾" diameter iron pipes
¾" diameter elbows
Construction adhesive (optional)
¾" pipe clamps
1" screws
Wire

Tools:
Pencil
Ruler
Compound miter saw or
    circular saw and scrap wood
Cordless drill with driving bit
⅛" diameter drill bit
120- and 220-grit sandpaper
Clean rag

1: Select a 2×12

At your local home improvement store, select one 2×12 that has minimal warping and the desired color of choice. You can have the store cut it in half to make it easier to transport. If you don't have the pieces cut for you, refer to the diagram.

2: Cut the pieces

Cut one 9-inch-long piece from each half of the 2×12 using the compound miter saw. If you need to use a circular saw instead, make sure to clamp a straight piece of wood to the piece you're cutting to use as a guide. You want right-angled cuts, and a clamped-on guide makes this easier. You should now have a top

piece, a bottom piece, and two side pieces. The pieces in each set should be equal in length or at least within ⅛" of each other.

3: Assemble the box

Using the 2½" screws and the cordless drill, screw through the long ends and into the edges of the short pieces. Do your best to keep the pieces perpendicular to each other.

4: Sand and finish the box

Sand the assembled box with 120-grit sand-paper followed by the 220-grit. Remove the dust using the clean rag and finish the wood with linseed oil or as desired.

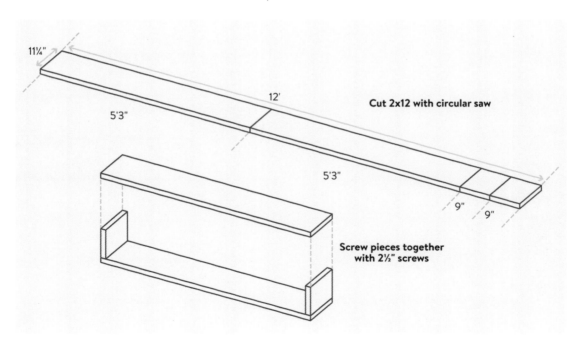

11¼"

12'

5'3"

Cut 2x12 with circular saw

5'3"

9"   9"

Screw pieces together
with 2½" screws

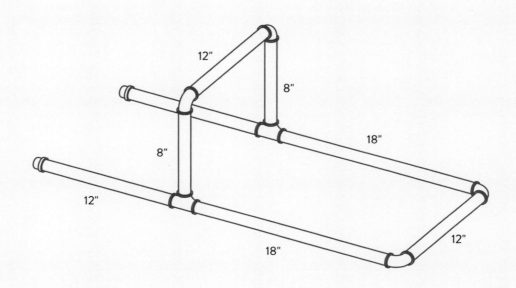

5: **Assemble the legs**

Screw the pipes together as shown in the diagram. When you get to the last cross bar (this is the tricky part), screw the 12" pipe into the 90-degree elbow completely. Then line up the opposite end with the other elbow and screw it in only halfway. The result will be a pipe that is only halfway screwed into each elbow. This assembly should be secure, but if you want to be extra safe, use some construction adhesive inside the elbow fittings.

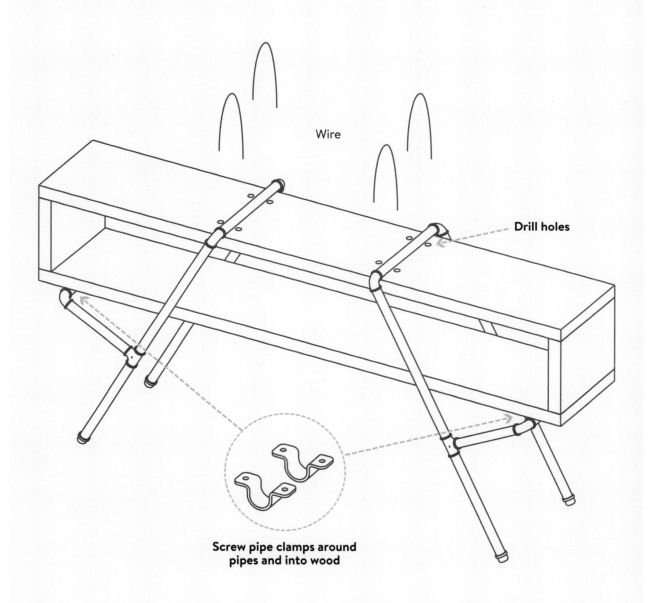

Wire

Drill holes

Screw pipe clamps around
pipes and into wood

6: Assemble

Slide the box between the pipes. Secure the pipe legs to the bench by adding pipe clamps fastened with 1" screws to the bottom pipe and the bottom of the wood box. For the upper part, drill two ⅛"-diameter holes and use pieces of wire to fasten the top pipe to the top of the wood box.

What can go wrong?

Warped wood!

2×12s are structural-grade lumber and aren't perfectly straight. There are different levels of warping, and a severely warped piece can make everything else difficult. Warped wood or uneven cutting and assembling can cause the entire piece not to sit flat. You can fix any wobbling by disassembling the box and trimming the ends more accurately or by screwing a different combination of pipes together to make adjustable feet for the bench. To do this, simply pair a short threaded pipe with a cap to make feet for the bench that adjust.

Alternatives

Change the look of the project by staining or painting the wood shelves.

What if you don't want it anymore?

If the project no longer works in your home, use it outside as a plant stand or as storage in your garage. Constructing this project does minimal damage to the materials, so you can always disassemble it and reuse the parts. The pipes can be reused as long as they're not rusty and the 2×12s only have screws at the ends, so even the wood box can be dismantled and repurposed.

Geometric Modular Plywood Coffee Table

A coffee table has many uses: footrest, magazine holder, and occasional dinner table. Make this modular set the centerpiece of your living room or split them up and use them around your house. This project is easy, versatile, and has a refined, mid-century modern aesthetic that will stand the test of time.

Estimated Time:

3 hours

Estimated Cost:

Under $100

Supplies:

1 4' × 8' sheet of ¾"-thick plywood (for easier transport, have it cut in half at the store)

1¼" screws

9 to **12** premade bench-height legs (about 12" to 18" high)

Acrylic finish for plywood with a low VOC such as Minwax

Tools:

Pencil

Ruler

Cordless drill with driving bit

Clamp

Straightedge

Circular saw with plywood blade

220-grit sandpaper

Clean rag

High-quality bristle brush

1: Mark the layout and double stack the plywood

The tabletops are made from ¾" plywood. Cut two equal size pieces of plywood with a circular saw or have Home Depot do it for you. This project can be made in a variety of different shape combinations, but if you like the one I made, you can print a template from HomeMade-Modern.com. If you want to create your own design, use a pencil and ruler to draw the desired shapes on the top piece of plywood.

2: Screw the pieces together

Lay the marked half of the plywood on top of the remaining piece, edges even. Screw the two pieces together using the cordless drill without worrying about the placement of the screws. If your screws end up on your cut lines, just remove the ones that are in the way. You don't need to put in all the screws yet, but add enough to hold the pieces together while you make the cuts.

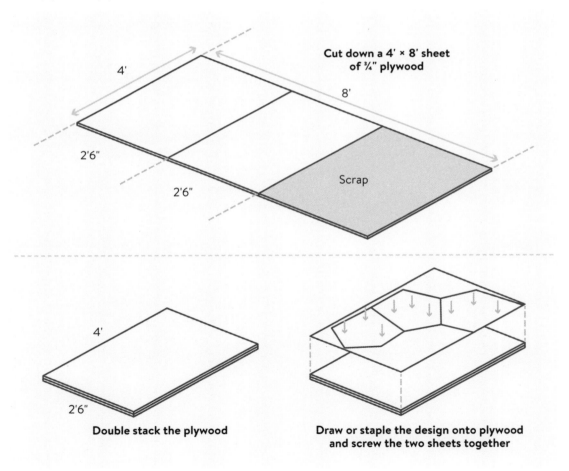

Cut down a 4' × 8' sheet of ¾" plywood

4'

8'

2'6"

2'6"

Scrap

4'

2'6"

Double stack the plywood

Draw or staple the design onto plywood and screw the two sheets together

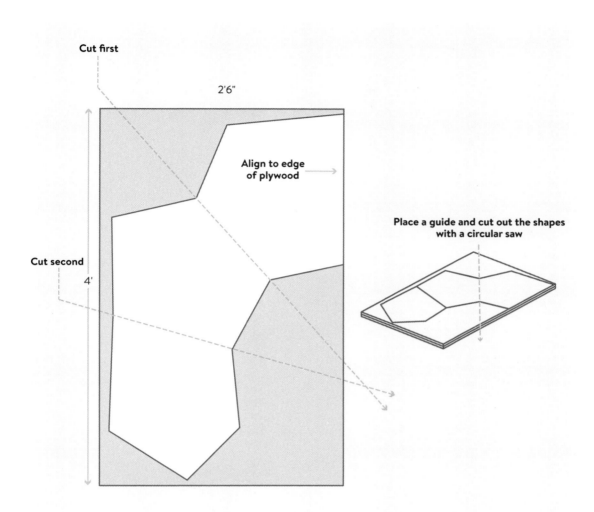

Cut first

2'6"

Align to edge
of plywood →

Place a guide and cut out the shapes
with a circular saw

Cut second

4'

3: Cut the pieces

Clamp a straightedge to the double-thick plywood and cut along the lines with a circular saw. (Before you start cutting, remove any screws that are on the cut lines.) A plywood blade is best for minimizing the tear to the bottom piece of plywood.

4: Add additional screws

Reinforce the tabletops by adding screws around the edges of each one.

Screw on hairpin legs

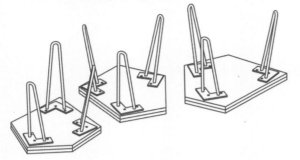

Flip over, sand, and finish

5: Sand the edges

Use 220-grit sandpaper to smooth the edges on the tabletops. Remove the dust using the clean rag.

6: Screw on the legs

Flip the tabletops upside down. Attach the legs to each using the screws and cordless drill.

7: Finish the tabletops

Apply the acrylic finish using a high-quality bristle brush. This type of brush will minimize bubbles and bristle shedding into the finish.

What can go wrong?

Not much. This project is easy.
Plywood makes a perfect tabletop since it's smooth and flat, and using premade legs is a great shortcut. This project is really about assembly. The one thing to look out for is gaps between the layers of plywood. To avoid this, be sure to firmly hold down the plywood pieces when screwing them together.

Alternatives

This project looks great in a variety of different colors, and plywood takes paint quite well. You can also do some really cool stenciling on the tabletop.

What if you don't want it anymore?

Simply disassemble it. The legs are reusable, and the plywood can be cut up to make smaller projects.

Crane Floor Lamp

Older homes and apartments don't always have built-in lighting in the places you need it. An adjustable floor lamp can provide a variety of options for adding additional light. This floor lamp made from electrical conduit and 2×3s is affordable, stylish, and can be built in different lengths. It can be used by itself with a simple cloth cord or dressed up with a pendant lampshade.

Estimated Time:
2 hours

Estimated Cost:
Less than $50

Supplies:
1 10' × ½" EMT conduit
1 8'-long 2×3
1" screws
Pendant fixture

Tools:
Pencil
Ruler
Tube cutter, hacksaw, or metal-cutting blade on the Ryobi with Multi-Tool Attachment
Vise grip pliers
Circular saw
Cordless drill with driving bit
¾" diameter drill bit
Knife or box cutter
120- and 220-grit sandpaper
Clean rag
Conduit bender

NOTE: My favorite place to buy inexpensive pendant fixtures is Color Cord Company. Its fixtures have cloth cords and come with a variety of plug, switch, and socket options in nearly every color imaginable.

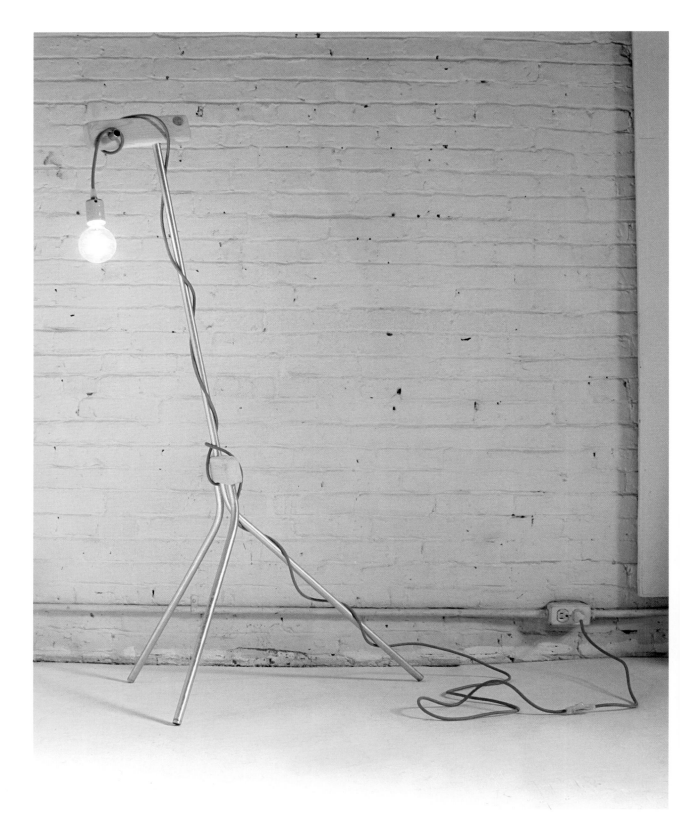

1: **Cut the conduit**

With the pencil and ruler, mark the EMT conduit as indicated in the diagram. Use a tube cutter and a pair of vice grip pliers. If you do not have a tube cutter, a reciprocating saw with a metal cutting blade will work. To cut the conduit, tighten the tube cutter around the conduit and use the pliers to grip it. Twist the cutter to create a score line. After a few rotations, tighten the cutter and repeat. Make multiple turns, cutting deeper each time. Once you have a deep score line all the way around, cleanly break off the conduit.

2: **Cut the 2×3**

Use the saw to cut the 2×3 as indicated in the diagram.

3: **Drill the holes**

Drilling holes at an angle is the trickiest part of this project, but conduit is a forgiving material that can be bent to hide your mistakes. Drill holes through each 2×3 using the cordless drill and ¾" bit. (See the diagram.)

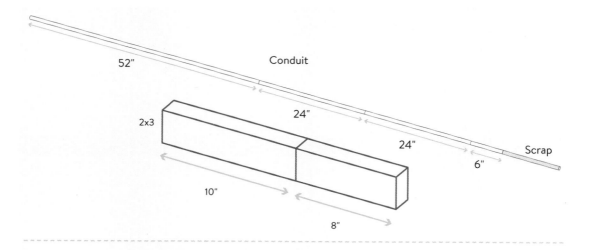

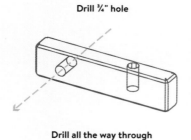

Drill ¾" hole

Drill all the way through

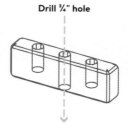

Drill ¾" hole

Drill all the way through

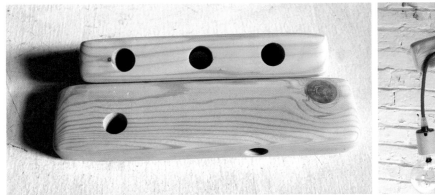

4: Carve and sand

2×3s can be turned into smooth blocks with curved edges with a little carving and sanding. Use the knife to shape the edges, then sand and smooth them with the 120-grit sandpaper followed by the 220-grit. Remove the dust with the clean rag.

5: Assemble

Bend the pieces of conduit with a conduit bender as shown in the diagram. If you don't have a bender, you can bend it by hand and use a scrap piece of 2×4 with a hole drilled in it to assist you. Slide the bent conduit through the holes and then insert some small screws through the wood into the legs to keep the conduit from sliding.

6: Add the pendant fixture

Wrap the cord around the structure, allowing the pendant to dangle from the top. Plug it in and you're ready to go!

What can go wrong?

The pieces don't fit.

If your holes are way off the mark, putting the lamp together can be difficult. The easiest way to fix this is to make the holes bigger, giving the

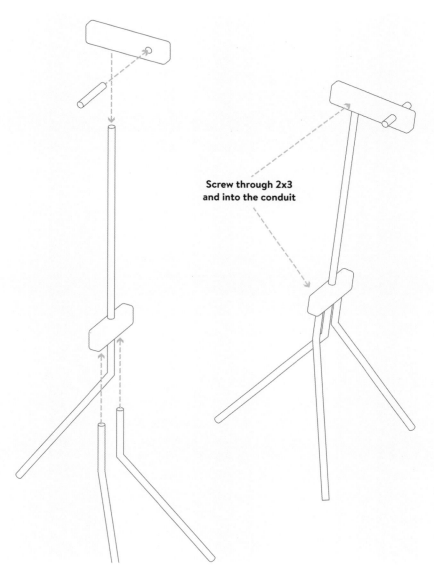

**Screw through 2x3
and into the conduit**

conduit wiggle room. There will be some visible gaps and you may need to use an extra screw or two to keep it all stable.

Alternatives
Change the entire look of the lamp by painting the conduit matte black, then pair it with a black cord and black porcelain socket.

What if you don't want it anymore?
If you no longer have use for the lamp, disassemble it and use the components to make a smaller version of the Garment Rack Closet Solution (see page 158).

Box Sofa and Daybed

Your sofa is probably one of the most expensive pieces of furniture you own. This wood-framed sofa is simple and durable, with a timeless style, and it can be built around almost any sofa cushions you might have, or even a single mattress if you want it to double as a daybed. I salvaged some cushions from an Ikea sofa whose frame had broken. Pile pillows along the sturdy, solid-wood sides and back to make this a perfect daybed for a couple to lounge on.

Estimated Time:
5 hours

Estimated Cost:
Under $250

Supplies:
5 8'-long 2×10s
4 8'-long 2×4s
2 8'-long 2×3s
3" screws
Dowels (optional)
2½" screws
#10 biscuits
L-brackets (optional)
Danish oil or low VOC latex paint (optional)
4 sofa cushions

Tools:
Ruler
Pencil
Compound miter saw
Orbital Sander
120- and 220-grit sandpaper
Clean rag
Biscuit joiner
Wood glue
Clamps
Cordless drill with driving bit
Paintbrush (optional)

1: Cut the 2×10s, 2×4s, and 2×3s

Measure, mark, and cut the 2×10s, 2×4s, and 2×3s into the lengths shown in the diagram using the ruler, pencil, and compound miter saw.

2: Sand the pieces

Sand the pieces with an orbital sander. Start with 120-grit sandpaper followed by the 220-grit. Remove the dust using the clean rag.

3: Assemble the panels

Lay the 2×10s for three panels on the floor. Use the biscuit joiner to cut notches in the 2×10s. Insert glue in the notches and then place a glue-covered biscuit in the notches. Use the pipe clamps to clamp the boards together while the glue dries.

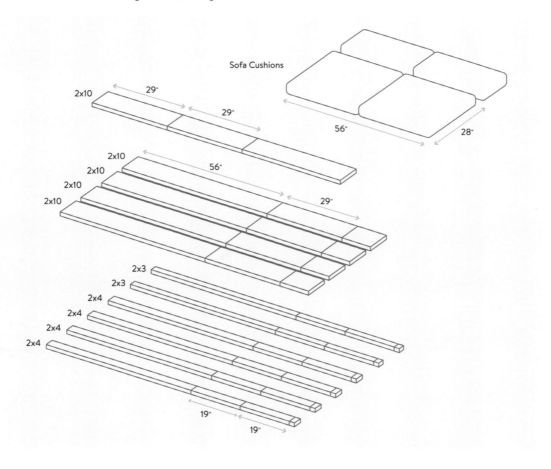

Sofa Cushions

2x10 29" 29"

2x10 56"

2x10

2x10

2x10 29"

56"

28"

2x3

2x3

2x4

2x4

2x4

2x4

19"

19"

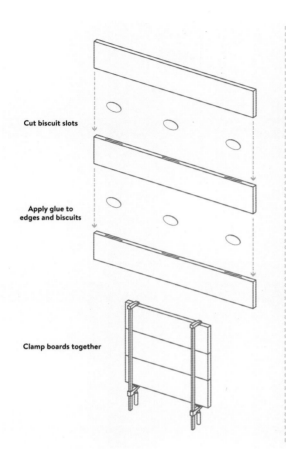

Cut biscuit slots

Apply glue to
edges and biscuits

Clamp boards together

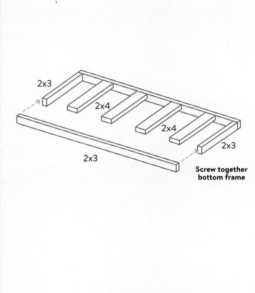

2x3

2x4

2x4

2x3

2x3

Screw together
bottom frame

4: Screw together the bottom frame

Assemble the bottom frame of the sofa using
the cordless drill and 3" screws.

5: Screw the frame to the panels

Screw the bottom frame to the back panel with
the top of the frame aligned with the top of the
first 2×10 in the panel.

6: Attach the side panels

The easiest way to attach the panels to the base is to screw them together. For a more finished look, align the screws, spacing them at even increments. If you want to go the extra mile, recess the screws, then cover them with wood plugs made from dowels. You'll probably need to add metal L-brackets on the inside for additional strength.

7: Finish

Paint the wood with a paintbrush or use Danish oil with a clean rag, if you like. I prefer to leave it raw, letting life add its own patina.

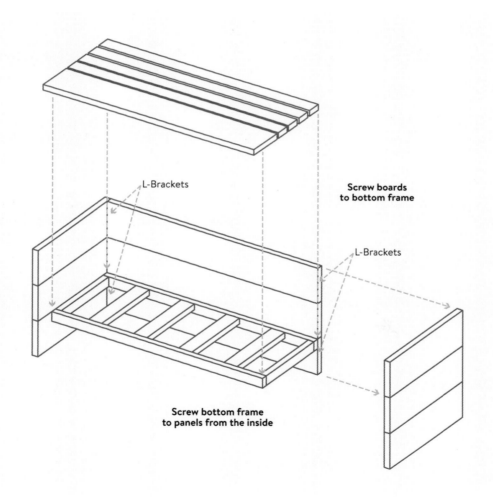

L-Brackets

Screw boards to bottom frame

L-Brackets

Screw bottom frame to panels from the inside

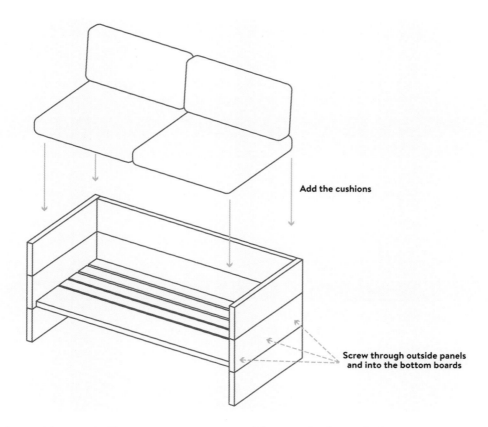

Add the cushions

**Screw through outside panels
and into the bottom boards**

8: Add the cushions and pillows

Set the cushions on the frame and add a bunch of pillows. Stockpile some snacks and you have the perfect fortress for a weekend-long Netflix binge!

What can go wrong?

The wood is warped.

Warping is a frequent issue with 2×10s, so select yours carefully. If you have trouble getting the corners to line up, try turning the panel upside down or changing how the pieces are arranged. If you have access to a thickness planer, plane the boards down a bit prior to assembling.

The wood splits with the screws.

Attach the screws slowly and carefully. If you hear or see the wood starting to crack and split, stop immediately and remove the screw. Pre-drill a hole, insert the screw, and try again.

Alternatives

You can experiment with painting the wood a different color. If this piece no longer works as a sofa or daybed, use it in a kid's room or guest room. It's the perfect size.

What if you don't want it anymore?

Disassemble it and use the wood for another project. Because you'll end up with large pieces of wood, you can easily use it to make one of the table or bookshelf projects.

Concrete Nesting Tables

Nesting tables are incredibly versatile pieces of furniture. Together, they can function as a coffee table, and apart, they make perfect side tables or night stands. I made these nesting tables using nothing more than Quikrete concrete and Lego bricks. I made the mold with Lego pieces after raiding my parents' attic to retrieve my childhood stash. I also purchased a few additional sets to round out my collection. See how these concrete tables show the texture from the Lego bricks? Let me show you how it's done.

Estimated Time:
6 hours plus curing time

Estimated Cost:
Under $25

Supplies:
Mold (should be built 23 layers high using mostly 2×4-dot Lego bricks)
1 baseplate that is 48 by 48 dots (using several smaller baseplates is easier to remove than a single large baseplate)
1 80-pound bag commercial-grade Quikrete Countertop Mix or Quikrete 5000 Concrete Mix

Tools:
Plastic mixing tray (or a large plastic bowl if you want to pour the concrete in layers)
Spoon
Stick or dowel
Long-nose pliers

NOTE: With the exception of the baseplate, no Lego bricks are harmed in the making of these tables, so you might be able to borrow some from your favorite Lego enthusiast and return them before he or she is home from school. Cleaning them, however, can be a bit time-consuming.

1: Construct the mold

Lay the baseplates on a clean, flat work surface. Don't try to use a single, large Lego baseplate because it will break when you try to remove it. Follow the diagram to build the Lego mold up brick by brick until you have a mold that is as high as you want your tabletop to be. I made my mold 23 layers tall. When you get to the top, add some cross support braces. I made the support braces out of a variety of 2×8 dot bricks. These braces keep the walls from bending out under the weight of the concrete.

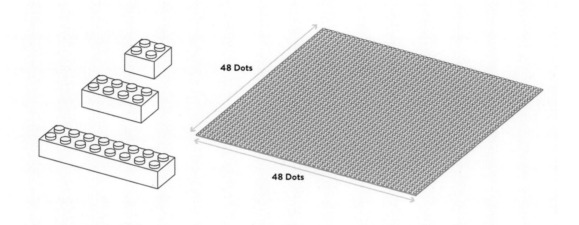

48 Dots

48 Dots

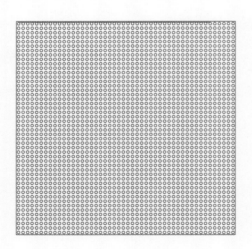

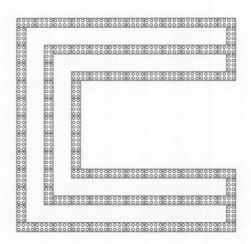

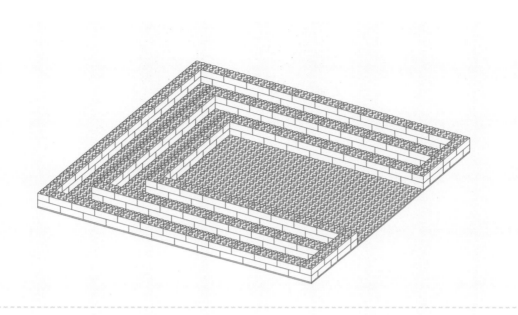

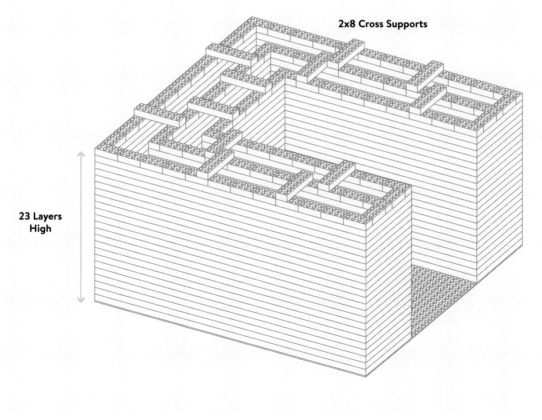

2x8 Cross Supports

23 Layers High

2: Mix and pour the concrete

Mix the concrete and water in a plastic mixing tray or a large plastic bowl. Different concrete mixes require different amounts of water, so refer to the manufacturer's recommendations for proportions. I used a large mixing tray so that I could pour it all at once, but it is possible to use a mixing bowl and pour it in layers. When it's the consistency of cookie dough, spoon it into the mold. When there is 3" of concrete in the bottom of the mold, use a stick to push the concrete into the corners. Move the stick in a repeated up and down motion to vibrate the concrete. The vibration of the concrete will push the air bubbles to the surface. Repeat this process until the mold is full. There is no need to smooth or level the concrete.

3: Let the concrete cure

The concrete needs to cure for at least 20 hours or per the manufacturer's recommendation before you remove the mold.

4: Remove the mold

Removing the Lego bricks can be a bit time-consuming. Start by removing a few of the top layers, then flip the entire piece over to remove the baseplates and additional layers. (It's easier to remove the bricks from the bottom.) You can use long-nose pliers to aid in their removal, but be careful not to scratch or bend the bricks.

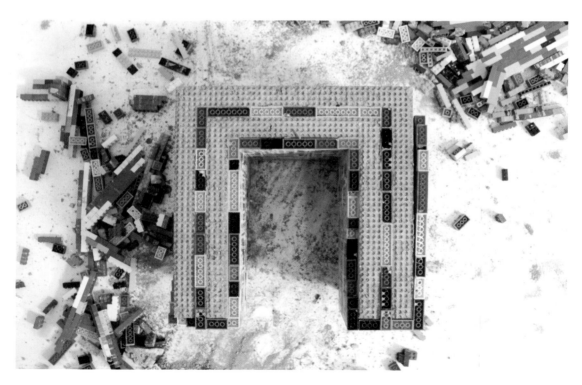

5: **Clean the Lego bricks**

Most of the dried concrete will flake off the Lego bricks. Any remaining pieces can be scraped or brushed with a toothbrush. Use cold water and a mild, non-abrasive soap to wash the bricks by hand or place the bricks in a mesh laundry bag and machine-wash them on cold. Do *not* use hot water or you will warp the bricks.

What can go wrong?

The Legos are stuck!

Removing the inner layer of Legos between the two tables can be frustrating. Take your time and use the long-nose pliers to carefully remove the bricks.

The concrete breaks!

Adding too much water when mixing the concrete can weaken it and lead to cracking and breaking after it dries. Be sure to always follow the manufacturer's directions. Thin applications of concrete can be delicate at first. Concrete does not reach its full strength until it has cured for weeks.

Alternatives

You can make these nesting tables in a variety of different sizes and proportions depending on how many Lego bricks you have access to. I made a pair of them, but by using the same technique you can make additional smaller tables that nest under the larger ones.

What if you don't want it anymore?

Concrete is not easily recycled, but these nesting tables are so versatile it shouldn't be hard to find them a new home. They can also be used outdoors and are great stands for potted plants.

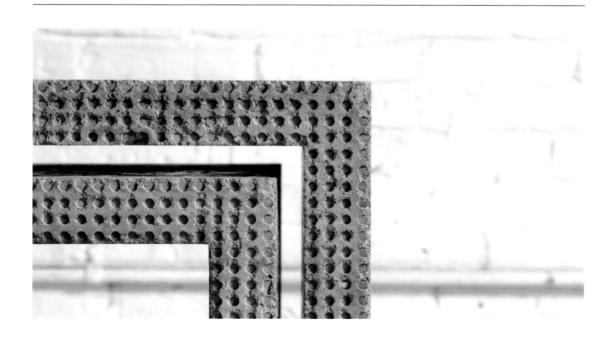

Ironbound Bookcase

Simple wood paired with black angle irons gives this bookcase a rustic, modern look. I don't use nails often, but for this project basic iron nails are the perfect accent. Because the bookcase is understated, it can work in virtually any room—in the dining room as a side bar, in the living room behind the sofa as a console table, in the home office, or even the bedroom.

Estimated Time:
4 hours

Estimated Cost:
Under $75

Supplies:
2 8'-long 2×10s
4 36" × 1½" angle irons
Lubricating oil for drilling
2 36" × 1½" fir square balusters
2" screws
Common nails with a flat broad head
Danish oil

Tools:
Ruler
Pencil
Compound miter saw
Drill bit for steel (use a drill bit
    that is slightly larger than the nails)
Drill press
Clamps
Orbital sander
220-grit sandpaper
Clean rag
Cordless drill with driving bit
Hammer

NOTES: If you don't have the bench-top tools I used to make this project, you can still make it using hand tools. Instead of the drill press and compound miter saw, you can use a cordless drill, circular saw, speed square, and clamps. To ensure square cuts, clamp the speed square to the wood first to guide the saw.

If you don't have any drilling oil on hand, you can use WD40, which isn't ideal, but it's better than nothing.

1: Cut the shelves

You can make this bookcase with either three or four shelves, but it's critical that the shelves are the same length. I cut the two 2×10s into two pieces each, all 4' long, using a compound miter saw to make accurate square cuts.

2: Cut the balusters into supports

Using the compound miter saw, cut the fir balusters into eight supports (one for both sides of each shelf), equal in length to the width of the 2×10s.

3: Mark the location of the holes

Using a pencil, mark all four angle irons to indicate the placement of where you would like the shelves. Then mark an "X" each place you'll need to drill a hole on the angle irons. For each shelf, mark a single hole that will align with the long side of the shelf. Then mark two holes, one on top of the other, which will align with the short side of the shelf. The top mark will be for the shelf and the bottom for the baluster supports.

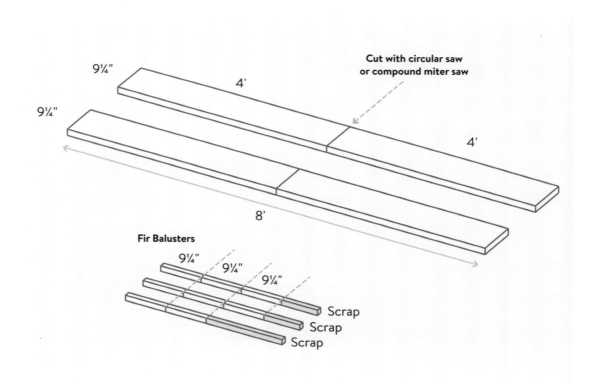

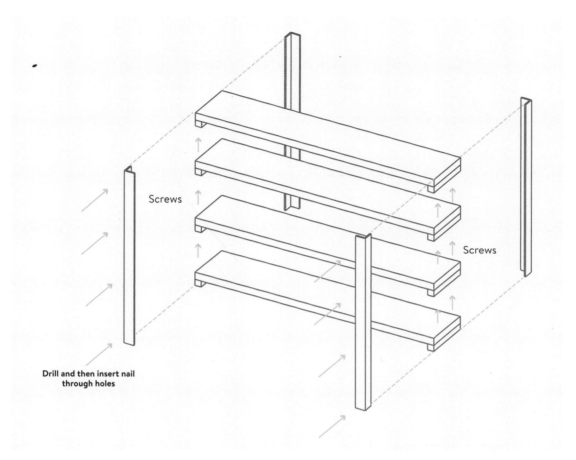

Screws

Screws

Drill and then insert nail
through holes

4: Drill through the angle irons

Drilling through steel is different than drilling through wood. Use only the drill bit specifically meant for steel and check your drill for the appropriate speed settings. Firmly clamp and secure one angle iron to your work surface. Add lubricating oil to the drilling location before you begin. Drill holes through each "X" marked on the angle irons using the drill press and bit, using a bit sized slightly larger than the nails you're using.

5: Sand the supports and the shelves.

Use the orbital sander and 220-grit sandpaper to sand the supports and the shelves. Additionally, the inside corners of the angle irons are not perfectly square and have a slight radius. Round the corners of each shelf using the orbital sander so that they fit into the angle irons. Remove the dust using the clean rag.

6: Screw the supports onto the shelves

Lay one shelf wrong side up. Place one baluster support on top at each short end. Use 2" screws and the cordless drill to secure them to the shelves. Repeat these steps to add two supports to each remaining shelf.

7: Nail the back angle irons to the shelves

Lay the two back angle irons on the floor. Position the bottom shelf and drive nails through the angle irons and into both short sides of the shelf using the hammer. Next, position the top shelf. Be sure it's flush with the top of the angle irons before securing it with nails. Now secure the two middle shelves.

8: Nail the front angle irons to the shelves

Place one front angle iron on the shelves and make sure it's properly aligned. Beginning at the bottom shelf, drive nails through the angle iron and into the short end of the shelf using the hammer. Position the remaining angle iron at the opposite end and repeat these steps to secure it. Next, align the top shelf and secure it with nails. You may need to use a clamp or a second set of hands to wrestle the wood into place. Secure the two middle shelves, then stand the whole thing up.

9: Drive nails through the remaining holes

Drive nails through the remaining open holes to secure the shelves.

10: Finish the wood

Use a clean rag to rub a coat of Danish oil into the wood to finish the piece.

What can go wrong?

Warped wood.

2×10s are affordable and look great, but they can be warped, creating shelves that are sturdy and functional but not perfectly square. As long as the top and bottom are flat, it doesn't matter if the shelves are slightly off. The angle irons will straighten them out slightly. And once they're filled with books and other objects, you won't even notice if they're crooked.

Alternatives

You can make a taller version by using longer angle irons. However, the higher it gets, the less stable it may be, so I recommend anchoring it to the wall to keep it from tipping over.

What if you don't want it anymore?

Pull out the nails and unscrew the baluster pieces to completely disassemble the bookcase. The wood shelves and iron can easily be reused for different projects.

Concrete Bucket Stool

This is the project that started it all, and my Concrete Bucket Stool still epitomizes exactly what I am trying to do at HomeMade Modern. It's durable, simple to make, and aesthetically pleasing. This stool looks like it could retail for $50, but you can make it for $5. All you do is mix the concrete right in the bucket, add three dowels for legs while it's still wet, and let it cure. When you remove it, there's no damage to the bucket, and you have your very own modern piece of furniture.

Estimated Time:
1 hour plus curing time

Estimated Cost:
Under $5

Supplies:
48"-long wooden dowel with a 1¼" diameter
Quikrete 5000 Concrete Mix
5-gallon plastic bucket with a smooth bottom
Concrete blocks or scrap wood
Plastic water bottle
White interior house paint in a semi-gloss finish with a low VOC, or as desired
4 copper pipe caps that have an interior diameter of about 1¼" (optional) (big enough to fit snugly on the end of the dowels)
Construction adhesive (optional)
Washers with an outer diameter between ¾" and 1⅛" (optional)

Tools:
Ruler
Pencil
Hand saw or circular saw
Measuring cup
Stick, hand shovel, or large mixing spoon
120-grit sandpaper

NOTE: A single 48-inch-long dowel is all you need to make three sturdy legs. Although I used 1¼-inch-diameter dowels for the legs, you can use 1-inch-diameter or 1½-inch-diameter dowels too. An alternative to using dowels for the legs is to use old tool handles.

1: Cut the legs

Cut the 48" dowel into three 16" pieces using the ruler, pencil, and either a hand saw or a circular saw.

2: Mix the concrete

Add 3" of dry concrete to the bottom of a clean, dry bucket. Follow the manufacturer's recommendation, or mix in approximately three cups of water and stir it thoroughly using a stick, hand shovel, or large mixing spoon until every grain is wet. Add additional water, as needed, until the mix is the consistency of cookie dough. (Don't overwater the concrete or it will become weak and crumble.)

3: Shake out the bubbles

Mixed concrete has air bubbles trapped inside. Shake and tap the bucket to bring the bubbles to the surface.

4: Place the legs

Once the concrete has settled and most of the air bubbles are out, place the three dowel legs into the bucket, one at a time, 1½" deep into the concrete mixture, then let them rest against the sides of the bucket.

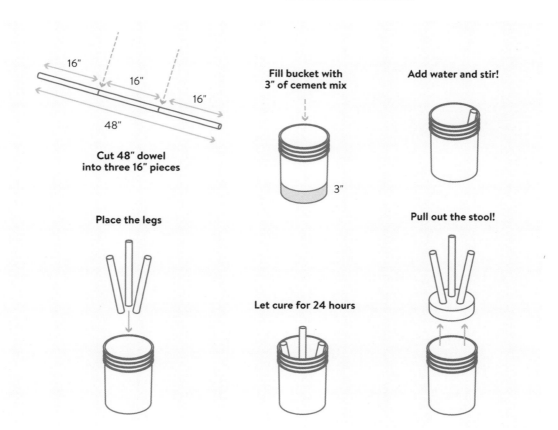

16"

16"

16"

48"

Cut 48" dowel into three 16" pieces

Fill bucket with 3" of cement mix

3"

Add water and stir!

Place the legs

Let cure for 24 hours

Pull out the stool!

5: Let the concrete cure

Wait 20 hours for the concrete to cure. Remove the bucket by bending the sides outward a few times in each direction to loosen the concrete, then pull the stool out by the legs.

6: Sand the edges

The concrete has not yet fully hardened and should be pretty easy to work with. Use 120-grit sandpaper to smooth the edges by hand.

7: Dip-dye the legs

Elevate the stool by placing it on top of concrete blocks or scrap wood to suspend the legs off the floor. Cut the top off the plastic water bottle and fill it with paint. Dip each leg into the bottle filled with paint. Allow the paint to dry completely.

Optional

8: Level out the legs with pipe caps

If your stool sits level on the floor, you're done. You can add pipe caps secured with construction adhesive to the bottom of each leg as a decorative element. Or, if one of the legs is shorter than the others, add a few washers to the cap before attaching it with the glue to make the leg even with the rest.

What can go wrong?

Uneven legs.

The legs can settle in the wet concrete unevenly. If this happens, trim them until they're level using a hand saw or multi-tool while the stool is still in the bucket. Use the rim of the bucket as a guide for how much to remove.

The concrete breaks.

If your concrete breaks, you either made it too thin, put the legs too close together or too close to the sides of the bucket, or added too much water. Thankfully, concrete is cheap, so if you mess up, use the legs again for your second try.

The stool sticks in the bucket.

This can happen if your bucket had a rough, scratched interior or was dirty prior to adding the concrete. Flex and bend the bucket to create separation between the walls of the bucket and the concrete. Adding water may help it slide out a bit, and if all else fails, use a heat gun to warm the bucket and soften the plastic.

Alternatives

Use other materials as molds. I used a square metal cake pan to make a 4-legged stool and added cross supports to the legs for additional strength. I used a silicon and glass round cake pan with commercial-grade, white Quikrete Countertop Mix to make a round version. This form worked incredibly well and left the concrete with a glassy, smooth finish. You can also add four longer legs and create a bar stool.

What if you don't want it anymore?

You can pull the legs out or cut them off to be reused for other projects. Turn the concrete seat into a paver or stepping stone in your yard.

DINING ROOM

Simple Plywood Table

This project is one of the easiest in this book because it's really more of an assembly project than a building project. It clearly illustrates the point that if you find great materials to put together, you can make amazing furniture. The fantastic thing about making your own furniture is that you can make it the exact size to fit your space.

Estimated Time:
3 hours

Estimated Cost:
Under $200

Supplies:
1 4' × 8' sheet of ¾"-thick PureBond birch veneer plywood
Wood glue
1¼" screws
4 28"-high trestle table legs in mint green
Minwax Polycrylic Protective Finish

Tools:
Ruler
Pencil
Clamps
Circular saw with plywood blade
Straight board to use as a guide (optional)
Cordless drill with driving bit
Orbital sander
120- and 220-grit sandpaper
Clean rag
Paintbrush

NOTES: I used PureBond plywood in a birch veneer, but any ¾-inch-thick plywood will work.
   Almost any premade table or desk legs would work for this project.
   Polycrylic Protective Finish is a protective topcoat for use on interior wood surfaces. It's great for protecting against normal wear and tear; it even resists water stains.

1: Cut the plywood

Use the ruler and pencil to measure and mark the cuts on the plywood. (See the diagram.) Cut the strips using the circular saw. I clamped a straight board to use as a guide for the long cuts.

2: Glue then screw the plywood together

Line up the edges of the support boards and apply a generous amount of wood glue. Hold the plywood in place with at least four clamps and use the cordless drill and 1¼" screws to securely fasten the two layers together. Arrange pieces (c), (b), (d), (e), and (f) atop piece (a) as shown in the diagram. Glue the support board pieces together at their edges using a generous amount of wood glue.

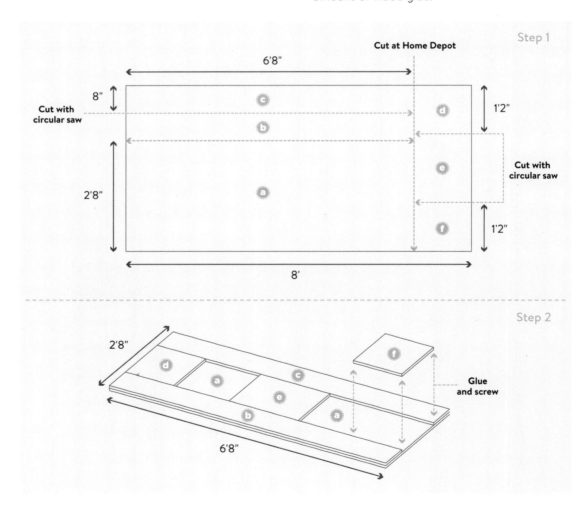

3: Sand the edges

Use the orbital sander to sand the edges of the plywood starting with the 120-grit sandpaper followed by the 220-grit. If you don't have an orbital sander, do it by hand. Remove the dust using the clean rag. If you were precise when lining up the edges, you won't need to do much sanding.

4: Screw on the legs

Lay the plywood wrong side up on your work surface. Attach one table leg to each corner using the cordless drill and 1¼" screws. Turn the table right side up.

6: Finish the tabletop

Using the paintbrush, apply two coats of the protective finish according to the manufacturer's instructions. Let dry.

What can go wrong?

There are gaps between the plywood layers.
Gaps can occur when the screw pushes up the top layer of wood when securing it. To prevent this, firmly hold the plywood down against the layer below while screwing.

Alternatives

If you're looking for a low-cost alternative for the legs, Ikea's Lerberg trestle table legs are durable with a clean aesthetic. The plywood tabletop can be painted or stained in a variety of different colors. You might even consider painting a pattern.

What if you don't want it anymore?

You can always switch out the legs and reuse the top or vice versa. When you're finished with the table, the legs can be reused to make a desk or other table and the plywood can be used for other projects.

Pipe Table

Rustic and industrial, this table will become the centerpiece of your domestic life for years to come. This versatile design looks just as fantastic in a bohemian art studio as it does in a modern loft. The solid-wood tabletop only gets better with age and will hold up against real life use—any nicks and scratches will just enhance the patina.

Estimated Time:
4 hours

Estimated Cost:
Under $250

Supplies:
12' to 20'-long 2×12s or 2×10s (depending on how warped the wood is and what sizes are available)

6 5"-wide × 2¾"-thick pieces of scrap wood or 6 straight bar steel brackets (I used scraps of ¾" pine)

1½" screws

12 ¾" black iron floor flanges

4 ¾" black iron 90-degree elbows

8 ¾" black iron T fittings

4 ¾" × 10" black iron pipes

4 ¾" × 18" black iron pipes

2 ¾" × 24" black iron pipes

12 ¾" × 3" black iron pipes

White or gray interior house paint in a matte finish (optional)

Bioshield Wood Counter Finish

Tools:
Ruler

Pencil

Circular saw (unnecessary if you purchase your wood cut to size)

Knife

Cordless drill with driving bit

Orbital sander

120- and 220-grit sandpaper

Clean rag

Paintbrush

NOTE: Iron plumbing pipes are a versatile DIY component that can be used to make just about any kind of structural support. The pipes I used to make this project yield a table that is slightly higher than average, which I prefer. To adjust the height, simply switch out the four vertical pipes between the T fittings. Iron pipes are not the cheapest material, but they will last a lifetime and can be repurposed over and over again.

1: Select the 2×12s

At your Home Depot, select two boards that have a nice grain and minimal warping. (2×12s are the most affordable solid lumber, but vary in look and finish.) For a longer table, I recommend using 8'-long 2×10s or 2×8s to minimize warping.

2: Cut the 2×12s

If you had your boards precut, proceed to step 3. Otherwise, measure, mark, and cut two lengths using the ruler, pencil, and circular saw. The lengths will depend on the size table you need to fit your space.

3: Lay out the boards and round the edges

Choose the sides of the boards that will serve as the tabletop and arrange their order. Round the outside edges of the short ends using the knife to give them a worn look.

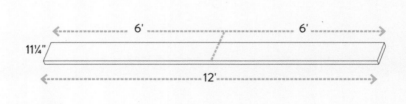

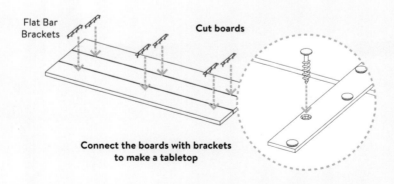

Flat Bar Brackets

Cut boards

Connect the boards with brackets to make a tabletop

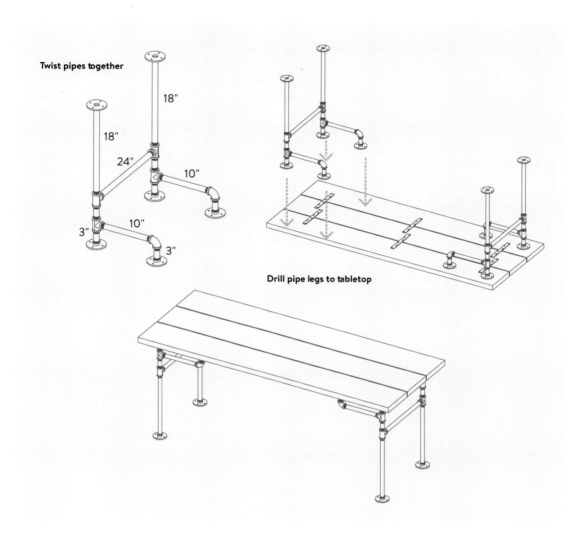

Twist pipes together

18"

18"

24"

10"

10"

3"

3"

Drill pipe legs to tabletop

4: Fasten the boards together

Turn the boards over, right sides down, keeping them in the same order and position. Use the scrap wood to connect the two boards together using the cordless drill and 1½" screws. 2×12s will never be completely flat, so do your best and don't worry if they're a little uneven.

5: Assemble the pipe legs

Screw the pipes together. Attach the assembled legs to the wrong side of the tabletop using the cordless drill and 1½" screws. You might have to adjust the pipes to get a relatively level surface. Turn the table right side up.

Sample 1

Sample 2

Sample 3

6: Sand

Sand the tables using the 120-grit sandpaper followed by the 220-grit. An orbital sander makes sanding a breeze, but doing it by hand works just as well. Remove the dust using the clean rag.

7: Finish the tabletop

Using a white or gray wash on the boards is a great way to give them an aged and weathered look. Make your own wash by diluting water-based interior house paint. The extra water thins the paint just enough to allow the wood grain to show through. Apply the coats using a paintbrush.

Sample 1: White Wash
Mix 1 part white paint with 4 parts water.

Sample 2: Wood Counter Finish
No stain or paint, just the wood sealer.

Sample 3: Gray Wash
Mix 1 part gray paint with 4 parts water.

8: Seal the tabletop
Regardless of whether you've applied a wash, seal the table using a natural wood counter finish like Bioshield per the manufacturer's recommendations. It is made from linseed oil and beeswax and provides protection without toxicity, which is important for surfaces that come in close contact with food.

What can go wrong?

The table isn't level.

Warped wood can result in a wobbly table. To fix this, adjust the length of the legs by unscrewing the pipe fittings a bit. Playing with how tightly they're screwed together should get you to the height you want. Another option is to slide a thin piece of wood between the top of the pipe leg and the underside of the tabletop.

Alternatives

Use premade legs! If pipes aren't your thing, try pairing the solid-wood tabletop with premade, table-height, steel, hairpin legs. Experiment with different paint colors and water-to-paint ratios. You can dilute water-based interior house paint as much or as little as you want. The more you thin it out with water, the more the wood grain will show through. I suggest trying the following on scrap wood to see which you might like: mix 1 part red paint with 6 parts water; mix 1 part red paint with 2 parts water; or red paint, no water.

What if you don't want it anymore?

You can unscrew the legs and turn the wood pieces into a media console.

Zipstitch Chair

Chairs are generally more difficult to make than benches or stools, but here's one that can be made by "stitching" plywood pieces with zip ties. I was able to make two chairs out of a single 4' by 8' sheet of plywood. It takes a little practice to become comfortable with using the zip ties so initially you might break a few; just be patient and you'll be stitching like a pro before you know it.

Estimated Time:
6 hours

Estimated Cost:
Under $25

Supplies:
1 4' × 8' sheet of ½"-thick plywood
4" zip ties
3' zip ties (for supports) or plywood scraps

Tools:
Ruler
Pencil
Circular saw with plywood blade
Clamps (optional)
Orbital sander
120- and 220-grit sandpaper
Clean rag
Cordless drill
¼"-diameter drill bit
Long-nose pliers
7"-long diagonal pliers

1: Measure and mark the plywood

Follow the diagram to measure and mark the plywood using a ruler and pencil.

2: Cut the pieces

Cut out the plywood pieces using the circular saw. If your saw doesn't have a laser guide,

which makes it easy to follow the drawn lines, clamp a guide to the plywood.

3: Sand the edges

Use the orbital sander to smooth the edges of the plywood pieces starting with the 120-grit sandpaper followed by the 220-grit. If you don't have an orbital sander, you can sand the pieces by hand. Remove the dust using the clean rag.

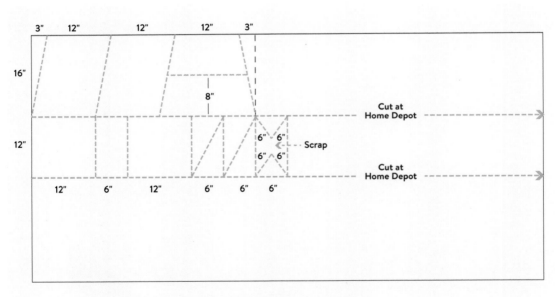

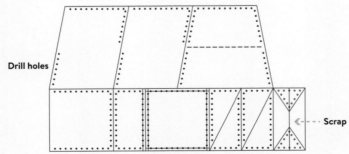

4: Mark the holes

Following the diagram for each particular piece of plywood, measure and mark a line ½" from the edges using a pencil. Mark an "X" at 1" intervals along the line to indicate where to drill the holes.

5: Drill the holes

Drill holes through each marked "X" using the cordless drill and ¼" bit. Although you can drill the holes through one piece of plywood at a time, I clamped two to three together and drilled the holes through multiple pieces simultaneously with "X"s aligned.

6: Loosely stitch the boards together

Start with the piece of plywood that will become the seat. Insert one zip tie through each drilled hole and secure the ends together making a loose loop. Now insert one zip tie through each drilled hole in an adjacent piece of plywood, but don't secure the ends until you've threaded each one through a corresponding loop in the first piece. This creates chain links of zip ties. Keep the links loose for now. Repeat these steps to attach the remaining pieces of plywood.

7: Shape and tighten

Shaping and tightening the zip ties is an incremental process that requires patience. The good news is you can always cut and redo them if you make a mistake. Use long-nose pliers to tighten the ties and diagonal pliers to trim away the excess.

8: Add supports

Use the 3' zip ties to make tension supports for the chair. On each side of the chair, drill two holes, ¼" apart. Use a box cutter to cut out the area between the holes until it's large enough to slip the zip tie through. Cut the head off a second zip tie to cap the opposite end. Use the same method to make vertical supports that keep the back from reclining too far. The exact location of these supports depends on how far back you want the chair to recline. Test out the chair first and then add these zip tie tension supports to set the maximum reclining point to exactly where you want it.

What can go wrong?

It looks crooked!

Assembling this chair is a bit tricky. The first time I made one it looked crooked. Then I realized that I threaded the zip ties differently on each side. To fix it, I had to clip off one side and restring it using all new zip ties.

Alternatives

You can paint or stain the plywood before assembling the chair. You can even play with patterns by only painting a few of the plywood pieces.

What if you don't want it anymore?

The plywood pieces are small, but since they're free of glue or hardware they can be salvaged for future projects.

Pendant Baseball Bat Lamp

I always found baseball boring, and I'm not into kitschy displays of Americana. So when a friend asked me if I could design something out of her son's old little league baseball bats, I looked for an idea that would highlight the form and material. Metal bats are made from high-performance aluminum alloys and have a streamlined form with no visible seams, which makes them perfect to transform into modern light fixtures. Used bats are quite inexpensive, so your sleek, well-made fixture will also cost you relatively little money.

Estimated Time:
3 hours

Estimated Cost:
Under $35

Supplies:
Metal baseball bat
Pendant light cord set with porcelain socket
Wine cork

Tools:
Ryobi JobPlus with Multi-Tool Attachment and
    metal-cutting blade or reciprocating saw
Cordless drill with paint-stripping wheel
    attachment
Knife
Long-nose pliers
Medium-grit sanding pad
Fine-grit sanding pad (optional)
Abrasive compound (optional)
Drum-sanding attachment for the cordless drill
Wire-brush attachment for the cordless drill
Pliers
Drill bit (big enough for the cord
    to fit through)

NOTES: Aluminum baseball bats can be found on eBay, Craigslist, or at thrift stores for about $4 apiece; this is a great price for a high-grade material like aluminum.

The Color Cord Company is my favorite place to get light fixtures. You can buy a pendant light cord set in virtually every color in the rainbow.

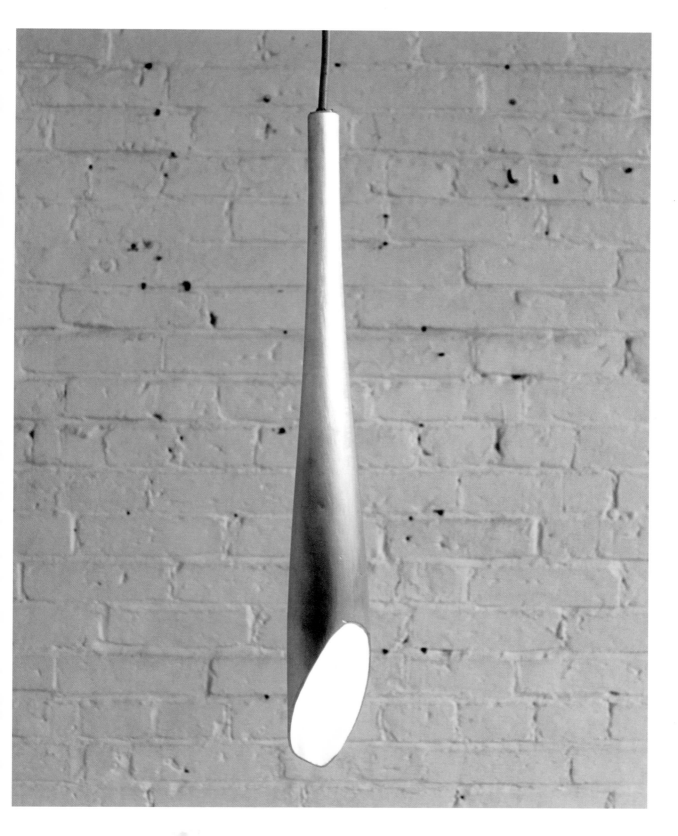

1: Cut the bat

If you like the look of the curved cut (see page 95), use the Ryobi JobPlus with Multi-Tool Attachment with the metal cutting blade to slice off the wide end of the bat at an angle. It takes about 5 to 10 minutes, but the Multi-Tool gives you great control over the angle, and the result is a beautiful curved line. If you want a clean, straight cut, use the reciprocating saw with the metal cutting blade. It goes through the baseball bat like butter. (If you don't have either power tool, you can use a hacksaw, but it will take a while.) Cut off approximately 2" of the opposite, knob end. Once you cut off both ends of the bat, you'll be left with a metal tube to serve as the lampshade.

2: Remove the paint

Most metal bats are partially painted. Remove the paint using the cordless drill and the paint-stripping wheel attachment.

3: Remove the foam

Some bats have foam inside them. Remove the foam by cutting it, then pulling it out using the knife and the pliers.

4: Sand the outside

Use the medium-grit sanding pad to sand the outside of the bat, giving the aluminum a shiny exterior. To get the look of brushed aluminum, sand the bat by hand in one direction. To get a mirror finish, sand the bat using the fine-grit sanding pad and then polish it with abrasive compound.

5: Sand the edges

Sand the cut edges of the bat until smooth using the cordless drill and drum-sanding attachment.

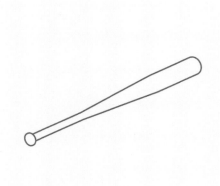

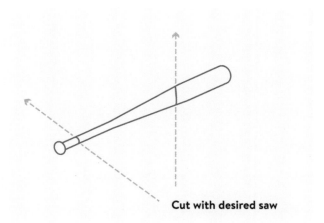

Cut with desired saw

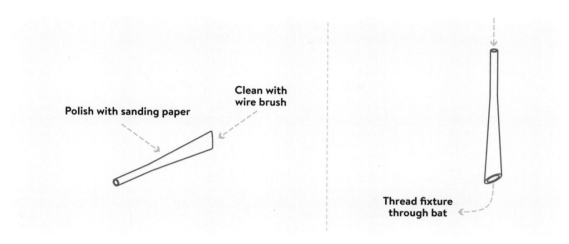

Polish with sanding paper

Clean with wire brush

Thread fixture through bat

6: Wire brush the inside

Clean the inside of the bat using the cordless drill and cone-shaped wire-brush attachment. The cone-shaped attachment is particularly good at reaching the inside surfaces of the bat.

7: Wire the lamp

Disassemble and remove the socket from the pendant light cord. Thread the cord through the bat, then reattach the socket to the cord. Please use safety precautions and follow the manufacturing instructions on the package.

8: Make a cork stopper

Place the wine cork vertically on your work surface. While holding the bottom of the cork steady with the pliers, drill a hole through the center from top to bottom. Cut the cork down so it fits snugly in the narrow end of the bat. To get the cork around the cord, use the knife to make a vertical incision to the center hole.

Open the cork at the cut and slide the cord inside. Position the cork on the cord a couple inches above the socket.

9: Assemble and hang

Pull the cord from the narrow end of the bat so that the socket moves into the bat and the cork stopper is wedged into place. Screw on the lightbulb, plug in the lamp, and turn it on!

What can go wrong?

The light bulb doesn't fit!

Not all bats are the same size, and larger light bulbs might not fit, depending on where you cut the bat. Thankfully, light bulbs and sockets come in different sizes too. You can always find a smaller one that's just right.

Alternatives

Paint it black. If shiny metal is a bit too futuristic for your taste, try a spray paint in a matte finish to totally change the look.

What if you don't want it anymore?

Because aluminum has a monetary value, you can take it to the scrap yard, make a tiny bit of cash, and the bat will have a new life.

Knit Bench

I love to experiment with my furniture-making by playing around with completely unexpected materials. In this case, a knitted sleeve creates a juxta-position of different textures—the soft yarn against the hard wood—and you end up with a more comfortable bench in the process. If you're an experienced sewer or knitter, I hope this project inspires you to think of other ways you can apply those skills to your furniture making. If you don't knit, consider teaming up with a friend who does. You make two wooden benches, while your friend makes two knitted sleeves, and you each end up with a completed project!

Estimated Time:
1 hour plus knitting time

Estimated Cost:
Under $85

Supplies:
1 8'-long 2×12 of premium fir construction lumber
Danish oil
4 16"-high hairpin bench legs in black
¾" wood screws
Washers (optional)

Tools:
Ruler
Pencil
Circular saw
Box cutter
Orbital sander
120- and 220-grit sandpaper
Clean rag
Cordless drill with driving bit

NOTE: The knit sleeve is created as a flat piece using four skeins of jumbo yarn (weight category 6) and a circular needle, and is worked in seed stitch. It is seamed together with a yarn lacing so you can slip it on and adjust it accordingly.

1: Cut the 2×12

Cut the 2×12 to 5'10" long using the circular saw or have it cut at Home Depot when you purchase it.

2: Carve the edges

Use the box cutter to round the edges of the wood.

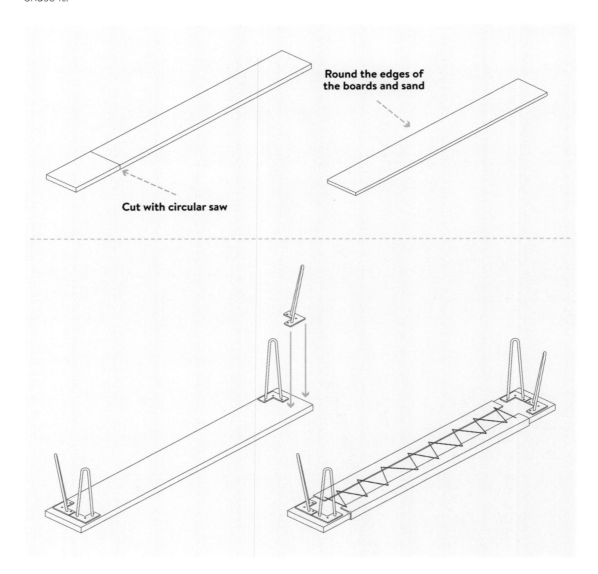

Round the edges of the boards and sand

Cut with circular saw

3: Sand the wood

Sand the 2×12 using the orbital sander with the 120-grit sandpaper followed by the 220-grit. Remove the dust using the clean rag.

4: Oil the wood

Apply one coat of Danish oil to the wood using the soft cotton cloth.

5: Attach the legs

Attach the hairpin legs to the wrong side of the wood using the cordless drill and screws. Turn the bench right side up.

6: Slide on the knitted sleeve

Loosen the lacing on the sleeve and slide it on over the legs. Then tighten and tie the lacings.

Tuck the ends under to hide them. (The sleeve is put on last so it doesn't get dirty while you attach the legs.)

What can go wrong?

Warped wood!

Warped wood can lead to all four legs not resting on the floor at the same time. This can be fixed by placing washers between the legs and the wood before securing them with screws.

Alternatives

Instead of a single, knitted sleeve you can add multiple knit cushions. If knitting isn't your thing, you can lash together knit scarves to assemble the sleeve. Of course, this bench also functions perfectly fine without a knitted sleeve.

What if you don't want it anymore?

Disassemble the bench and use the materials for other projects. Because the finished project is constructed with a large, solid piece of wood, you'll be able to use it for many other projects. You can use the legs on other benches. They're also perfect for a coffee table. Make knit cushions out of the cover.

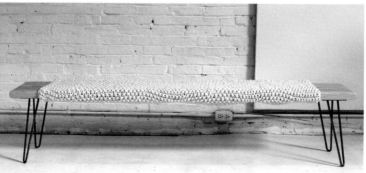

KITCHEN

Concrete Kitchen Island

This kitchen island is a like a workbench for your kitchen. The heavy-duty concrete countertop provides extra counter space, and the bottom shelf can easily store large pots and pans. I used gray Quikrete Commercial Grade Countertop Mix cast into a melamine form to make the top. It's as smooth and hard as stone and weighs about two hundred pounds. Even though the wood bottom looks intricate, it's actually quite easy to make. Only a few cross cuts are required, and it's assembled using stainless steel screws.

Estimated Time:
8 hours plus curing time

Estimated Cost:
Under $150

Supplies:
2 2' × 4' sheets of ¾"-thick melamine board
2½" stainless steel screws
⅝" stainless steel screws
Latex or silicone caulk
2 ½" × 36" pieces of rebar
2 ½" × 12" pieces of rebar
8-, 10-, 12-, or 14-gauge wire
3 80-pound bags of commercial-grade Quikrete Countertop Mix in gray
1 1" × 4" of scrap wood to screed the top of the concrete (should be at least 30" long)
4 8'-long 2×4s of cedar or premium construction lumber
3 8'-long 1×4s of cedar or premium construction lumber
1⅝" stainless steel screws
2½" stainless steel screws
3" stainless steel screws
Scrap wood pieces of 2×2s or 2×4s
Construction adhesive (optional)
Quikrete Acrylic Concrete Cure and Seal in satin finish

Tools:
Ruler
Pencil
Circular saw or compound miter saw
Cordless drill with driving bit
Hot glue gun and glue sticks
Clean rag
Wire clippers or pliers
Hoe
Large mixing tray or tub
Shovel
Stick (optional)
Speed square
220-grit sandpaper
Paintbrush

NOTES: Melamine board is particleboard with a smooth, laminate surface. It's a great product for making concrete formwork.

This project requires four to eight pieces of cedar. The range depends on how straight your pieces of wood are. If they're quite warped, you may have more waste. If cedar is too expensive for you (it costs a bit more than other softwoods), you can make this same design using standard 2×4s of any other construction lumber.

Stainless steel screws won't rust, which gives you the flexibility to move this project outside. Don't want to spring for the money? A cheaper option is to use deck screws.

1: Cut one melamine board into strips

Measure, mark, and cut three 2½" × 4' strips from one melamine board using the ruler, pencil, and circular saw. Set two aside. Cut the third strip as shown in the diagram. Set these aside.

2: Screw on the scrap pieces of 2×2 or 2×4

Lay the remaining 2' × 4' piece of melamine board flat on the floor. (This is the base of your formwork. The strips cut in step 1 will become the walls of your formwork in the next step.) To create supports for the walls, use the circular saw to cut the scrap pieces into six pieces approximately 5 to 6" in width. Position the cut pieces of baluster around the outside edges of the 2' × 4' piece of melamine, one in the center of each short side and two in the corners of each long side, as shown. Secure the scrap pieces to the melamine base using the cordless drill and 1⅝" screws.

3: Screw on the melamine walls

Position one 4'-long melamine strip directly in front of the scrap pieces on one long side of the melamine base. Position the second 4'-long melamine strip directly in front of the baluster supports on the opposite long side. To complete the four walls of the formwork, position the shorter melamine strips directly in front of the scrap pieces on each short side.

4: Glue down the formwork

Use the hot glue gun to adhere each melamine strip to the base and to the scrap pieces. Using hot glue will create a waterproof seal around the outside of the form. Making the concrete top is similar to the top we made for the Geometric Modular Plywood Coffee Table (see pages 47–49).

5: Seal and clean the formwork

Squeeze a bead of caulk into one corner and smooth it out along the joint with your finger. Repeat this step to seal every joint on the interior of the formwork with caulk. Let it dry. Remove all dust and dirt from the formwork before pouring the concrete.

6: Prepare the rebar

To make a rectangular reinforcement frame for the concrete, position the four pieces of rebar on your work surface so that they resemble a "#," placing equal lengths parallel to each other. Lash the pieces together where they cross using the wire and wire clippers or pliers.

7: Mix and pour the concrete

Following the manufacturer's directions, use a hoe to mix together approximately two and a half bags of Quikrete Countertop Mix with

Make the concrete top first before measuring and cutting the wood for the base. The concrete should overhang the base by at least ½".

STEP 2

Cut the wood.

CUT LIST:

a	2x4 – 39"	x 2
b	2x4 – 14"	x 2
c	2x4 – 30"	x 4
d	1x4 Field Measure (d) Pieces	x 4
e	2x4 – 36½"	x 2
f	1x4 – 14"	x 2
g	1x4 – 36½"	x 3
h	2x4 – 11"	x 3

STEP 3

Screw together the bottom tray.

STEP 4

Screw together the top frame and legs.

STEP 5

Slide the bottom tray between the legs.

STEP 6

Raise the bottom tray up 3½".

STEP 7

Screw through the legs into the bottom tray.

STEP 8

Take field measurements for the top trim (d) pieces.

STEP 9

Cut the trim pieces and screw them into place.

STEP 10

Lift the concrete into place and connect with construction adhesive or screw through (a) pieces.

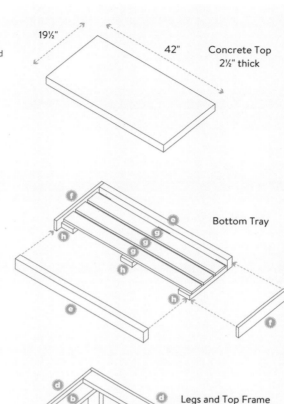

Concrete Top
2½" thick

19½"

42"

Bottom Tray

Legs and Top Frame

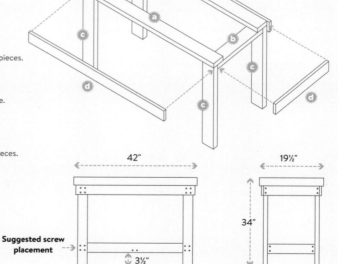

42"

19½"

34"

Suggested screw placement

3½"

clean water in a concrete mixing tray or tub. Follow the manufacturer's instructions for the amount of water you should use. This mix sets very fast, so work quickly. Use a shovel to fill the formwork about two-thirds full, place the rebar in the concrete, and fill it up the rest of the way.

8: Pack down the concrete and vibrate the form

Use a gloved hand or stick to pack down the wet concrete, especially in the corners. Tap on the formwork to vibrate it, which will remove the air bubbles. Level the concrete using the scrap wood 1×4 as a screed (a flat board used to smooth a concrete surface).

9: Let the concrete cure

Let the concrete cure for at least 48 hours before removing the formwork. The manufacturer also suggests covering the concrete to control the moisture levels.

10: Remove the formwork

Unscrew the scrap pieces using the cordless drill and remove the melamine walls. After you remove the formwork, scrape off any caulk stuck to the concrete. Set the concrete countertop aside until you construct the wooden island.

11: Cut the 2×4s

Cut the following from the cedar 2×4s using the circular saw and speed square: (a) two 39"-long pieces, (b) two 14"-long pieces, (c) four 30"-long pieces, (e) two 36½"-long pieces, and (h) three 12½"-long pieces. (You can also cut

the wood using the compound miter saw, which is easier.) Lightly sand all the rough edges using the 220-grit sandpaper.

12: Cut the 1×4s

Cut the following from the cedar 1×4s using the circular saw and speed square: (d) four pieces that need to be field measured in step 18 before cutting, (f) two 14"-long pieces, and (g) three 36½"-long pieces. (You can also cut the wood using the compound miter saw, which is easier.) Lightly sand all the rough edges using the 220-grit sandpaper.

13: Assemble the bottom tray

Follow the diagram to arrange wood pieces (e), (f), (g), and (h) for the bottom tray. Secure them together using the cordless drill and 1⅝" screws. Use the speed square to ensure that the corners are at 90-degree angles.

14: Assemble the top frame

Follow the diagram to arrange wood pieces (a) and (b) for the top frame. Secure them together using the cordless drill and 2½" screws. (The legs will complete the corners of the frame, so use a small piece of 2×4 as a stand-in until you're ready to attach the legs in the next step.)

15: Screw on the legs

Follow the diagram to position the legs (c) on the top frame. Secure them together using the cordless drill and 3" screws. Without the bottom tray to hold them in place, they will wobble a bit, so don't worry about making them square yet.

16: Screw in the bottom tray

Flip the top frame and legs right side up. Position the bottom tray between the legs. Slide two scrap 2×4s underneath the tray to raise it 3½ inches off the ground. Use the speed square to make sure the legs are in their correct positions, then use four 3" screws in each leg to secure them to the tray using the cordless drill.

17: Add additional screws

Now that the bottom tray is in place, drive additional 3" screws through the top frame and into the legs.

18: Cut and screw the top trim pieces

Measure the short sides of the top frame. Cut two pieces to that exact length from the cedar 1×4s using the circular saw and speed square. Follow the diagram to position these trim pieces (d) on the top frame. Secure them using the cordless drill and 3" screws. Repeat these steps to measure, cut, and screw two additional pieces from the cedar 1×4s to the long sides of the top frame.

19: Put on the countertop

The concrete top is heavy and shouldn't slide, but for extra security, add a few 2½" screws from underneath the top frame, through the wood and into the concrete, about ⅜".

20: Seal the concrete

Apply one coat of Quikrete Acrylic Concrete Cure and Seal using a paintbrush to protect and finish the concrete countertop.

What can go wrong?

It wobbles!

If the legs aren't the same lengths or you didn't square the legs as you screwed them on, the table could wobble. You can flip it upside down and sand down the legs until they're even.

Alternatives

Create an outdoor kitchen! You can build an outdoor version as long as your island is made with wood that weathers well, such as cedar or redwood.

What if you don't want it anymore?

Move it outside to use as a potting table or into the garage to use as a work bench. You can also reduce the weight by using a premade stainless-steel or wood top.

Pipe and Board Shelving System

You can find rustic industrial shelving like this one in chain furniture stores ranging from hundreds to well over one thousand dollars. This DIY version will cost you less than $200, and you can do the entire project in an afternoon. Your biggest financial outlay will be in purchasing the pipes needed, but they will last forever and can be disassembled, moved, and reinstalled in almost any setting, from a full height bookcase in a study to dry goods storage in a kitchen, or even as a closet organization system.

Estimated Time:
3 hours

Estimated Cost:
Under $200

Supplies:
½"-diameter black iron 90-degree elbows
½"-diameter black iron tees
½"-diameter black iron couplings
½"-diameter black iron floor flanges
½" × 8" black iron pipes
½" × 10" black iron pipes
½" × 12" black iron pipes
½" × 18" black iron pipes
Drywall anchors (optional)
½" wood screws
4 8" × 6' pieces of ¾"-thick pine
Danish oil
Pipe hangers (two per connection between pipe and shelves; I used 24)

Tools:
Level
Cordless drill
Ruler
Pencil
Circular saw
Orbital sander
220-grit sandpaper
Clean rag

NOTES: Home Depot has a great selection of pre-threaded pipes, and you should be able to make this project without having pipes custom cut and threaded. If you want to make a longer shelving system than this one, be sure to use pipe supports at least every three feet.

The length of the boards will vary depending on the size of the space you're trying to fill. Buy the specific size that works for you.

1: Assemble the pipes

Follow the diagram to screw the pipe pieces together to make pipe supports. I recommend putting a support at least every three feet of shelf length. They don't need to be super-tightly screwed together, just securely connected.

2: Screw the flanges to the wall

Space the pipe supports between 18" and 36" apart (I placed them 30" apart). Use a level to ensure the supports are vertical before securing the flanges to the wall using the cordless drill and screws. The length of the screws will

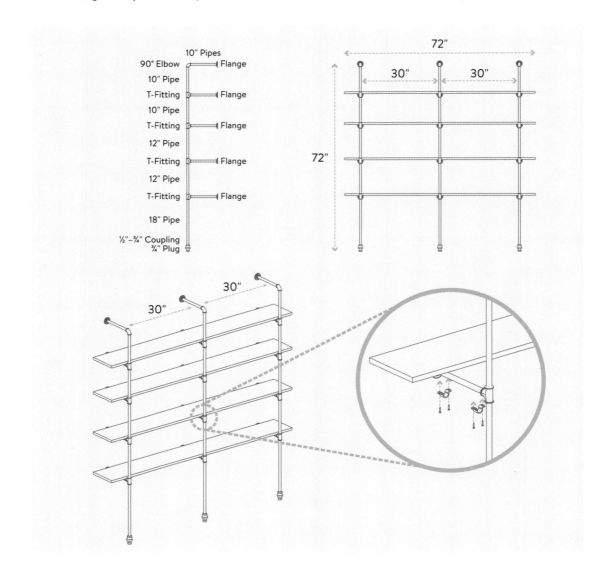

depend on your wall; the important thing is to make sure you have a secure connection. If your walls are made from gypsum board (drywall), use drywall anchors.

3: Cut the shelves

Measure, mark, and cut the shelves using the ruler, pencil, and circular saw. (For a longer shelving system, the shelves should overhang the end pipes about 2" on both ends.)

4: Sand and finish the shelves

Sand the shelves using the orbital sander and 220-grit sandpaper. Remove the dust using the tack cloth. Finish the shelves by applying one coat of Danish oil using the clean cloth rag.

5: Secure the shelves

Position the shelves on the pipe supports. Follow the diagram to secure the shelves in place using two pipe hangers per board, the cordless drill, and the ½" screws. (Pipe hangers are metal loops that are wrapped around the pipes and screwed to the underside of the shelves to secure them together.)

What can go wrong?

The shelves pull out from the wall.

There is a chance that your shelves can pull out from the wall if you haven't anchored them properly to support the weight. To prevent this, use drywall anchors or use a stud finder to attach them directly to the studs.

Alternatives

There are lots of different ways to make shelves with pipes. Some people like to drill holes in the boards and have the pipes go through them. I think it's a more integrated look, but they're harder to make and it limits the possible reuse of the materials. To change the look of the shelves, try finishing them with stain, in addition to the Danish oil, or simply paint them.

What if you don't want it anymore?

Disassemble the shelves and reuse the materials for other projects.

Pipe and Wood Bar Stool

These rustic, industrial bar stools can turn any counter into an eating area. Because you make them yourself, you can customize them to a variety of different heights for countertops and tabletops. I like to make them a little wider in the seat than the normal bar stool so that they're more comfortable.

Estimated Time:
4 hours

Estimated Cost:
Under $60

Supplies:
1 8'-long 2×4
1 8'-long 2×3
1 8'-long 2×2
Wood glue
8 ½"-diameter black iron 90-degree elbows
2 ½"-diameter black iron couplings
2 ½" × 6" black iron pipes
2 ½" × 3" black iron pipes
4 ½" × 12" black iron pipes
3 ½" × 14" black iron pipes
Danish oil

Tools:
Ruler
Pencil
Circular saw
Cordless drill
¾"-diameter drill bit
Clamps
Orbital sander
80-, 150-, and 220-grit sandpaper
Clean rag

1: Cut the 2×3 and 1×3

Measure, mark, and cut the 2×3 into 18" lengths and the 1×3 into 18" lengths using the ruler, pencil, and circular saw.

2: Drill through the 2×3s and 1×3s

For every 18" piece of wood, drill a hole about 4 inches in from each short end using the cordless drill and ¾" bit through the side of the piece.

3: Glue the wood together

Use wood glue to arrange the cut pieces into a wood block for the seat that is 18" by 11½" by 1½". Clamp the wood together and put one pipe through each hole to keep the block aligned while the glue dries.

4: Sand the block of wood

Shape the block of wood using the orbital sander and 80-grit sandpaper, followed by the 150-grit and 220-grit sandpapers to make it smooth. Remove the dust using the clean rag.

5: Assemble the pipes

Follow the diagram to assemble the pipes. Be sure to insert the short pipes connected to the elbows prior to assembling the legs.

6: Finish the wood

Apply one coat of Danish oil to the wood using the cloth rag.

What can go wrong?

The stool could be a little wobbly.
You can make adjustable legs by screwing together a different combination of pipes.

Alternatives

You can change the look of the project by staining the seat or adjusting the height of the barstools to work with a higher or lower counter by using longer or shorter pipes.

What if you don't want it anymore?

You can disassemble it and turn it into a table, or use the pipes for other projects in this book. With the addition of a bracket, the seats can be turned into small wall shelves.

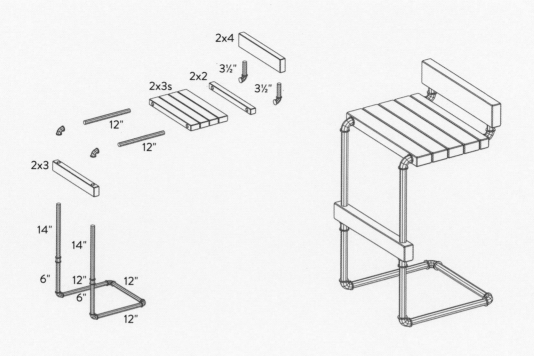

2x4

3½"

2x2

2x3s

3½"

12"

12"

2x3

14"

14"

6"

12"

6"

12"

12"

Height Options

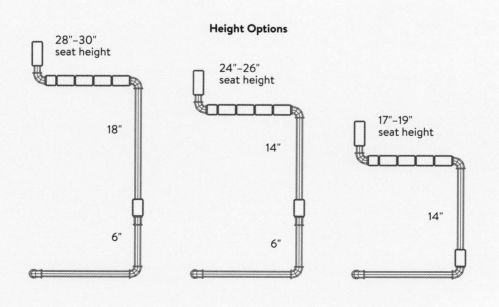

28"–30"
seat height

18"

6"

24"–26"
seat height

14"

6"

17"–19"
seat height

14"

Herb Garden Wall

This DIY vertical garden is an easy-to-make project that can turn any wall into a beautiful and productive herb garden. Who said you need a lot of space to have a garden? This project is perfect for the land-challenged. Simply hang this in front of a south-facing window and you have an easily accessible indoor greenhouse. You can even hang this from an awning or balcony to ensure privacy.

Estimate Time:
3 hours

Estimated Cost:
Under $40

Supplies:
3 8" × 6' boards of ¾"-thick pine
20 4"- to 5"-diameter terra cotta flowerpots
100' of ¼"-diameter rope
60 to **75** 4"-long zip ties

Tools:
Ruler
Pencil
Circular saw
Cordless drill
⅛"-diameter drill bit (I used a ⅛" bit, but you
    can use any metric or standard bit that's
    between ¹⁄₃₂" and ¼")
Clamps
4" hole saw attachment for the cordless drill
⁵⁄₁₆"-diameter drill bit
Orbital sander
220-grit sandpaper
Clean rag
Scissors or knife
Level
Diagonal pliers

NOTES: The rope I used was actually a clothes-
line. All 100 feet cost only $10.
    A hole saw is a drill attachment that cuts
large holes. Its ring-shaped saw blade attaches
to an arbor, and the arbor holds a drill bit to
bore a centering hole. To match a flowerpot
with the right size hole saw, choose a saw
with a diameter half an inch smaller than the
diameter of the pot.

1: Cut the boards

Measure, mark, and cut the pine boards in half using the ruler, pencil, and circular saw. Set one 3' board aside. (I only used five boards, saving the sixth one for another project.)

2: Mark the position of the holes for the flowerpots and ropes

On one board, use the pencil to mark the position of the holes for a row of four flowerpots, leaving approximately 2" between each one.

Then mark the position of the holes for the rope, one in each corner, 1" from the edges.

3: Drill pilot holes

The key to this project is making sure the holes are aligned. To help accomplish this, stack the boards, one on top of the other, edges even, with the marked board from step 2 on top. Drill pilot holes in the center of each marked flowerpot position and through the entire stack of boards using the cordless drill and 1/8" bit. These small holes will serve as guides for the hole saw. (Of course, if you'd rather mark each board individually you can do that too.)

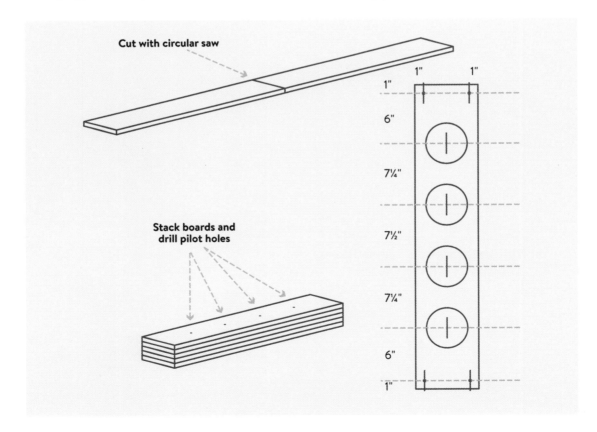

Cut with circular saw

Stack boards and drill pilot holes

1" 1"
1"
6"
7¼"
7½"
7¼"
6"
1"

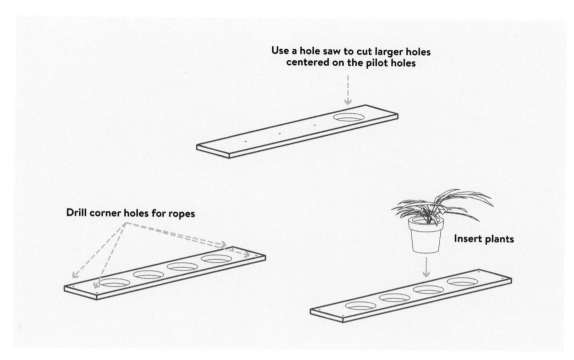

Use a hole saw to cut larger holes centered on the pilot holes

Drill corner holes for ropes

Insert plants

4: Cut holes for the flowerpots

Clamp the boards together, two at a time, to your work surface. Attach your hole saw to your cordless drill. Set it to drilling mode at the highest speed. With a firm grip on the drill and using both hands (hole saws can be tricky to handle), keep the drill perpendicular to the boards and drill the holes. (The larger diameter hole saws can generate a lot of friction, so it's important to properly secure the boards and have a firm grip on the drill. The saw will occasionally freeze up and bind against the wood, so be patient and be careful when you're using it.)

5: Drill holes for rope

With the boards still clamped together from step 4, drill the holes for the rope using the cordless drill and the 5⁄16" bit. (It's important to have a tight fit for the rope so that the zip ties create a stopper that keeps the boards from sliding.) Repeat steps 4 and 5 to drill the holes in the three remaining boards.

6: Sand the boards

Sand the boards using the orbital sander and 220-grit sandpaper. Since pine is a softwood, you can also hand sand them pretty quickly if you don't have an orbital sander. Remove the dust using the clean rag.

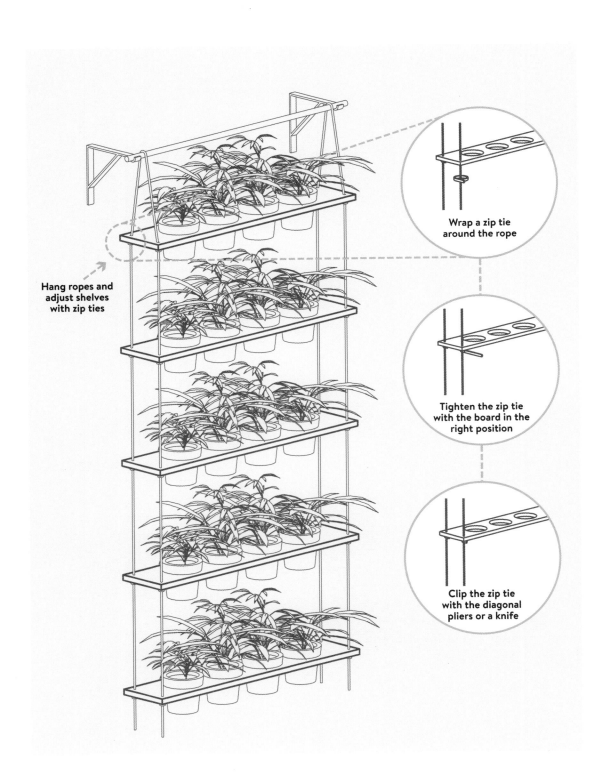

Hang ropes and
adjust shelves
with zip ties

Wrap a zip tie
around the rope

Tighten the zip tie
with the board in the
right position

Clip the zip tie
with the diagonal
pliers or a knife

7: String the boards

Cut the rope into four equal lengths using scissors or a knife. Thread the ropes through the corner holes and tie knots at the bottom of each length to secure them.

8: Hang the garden

Hang the garden from a location that can support the weight. (Closet shelf brackets work well.) When selecting a hardware system for hanging your garden, be sure to consider the weight of the garden when the soil is wet. I used closet rod brackets and wooden closet rods for mine. I screwed the closet rod brackets through drywall and into the studs of the wall. Then I placed the wooden rod on the brackets and then tied the ropes to it.

9: Secure the boards

Make sure you have adequate space for the plants between the boards. My boards were 10" apart, but yours can be different depending on the height of the plants that you plan on using. Slide the first board up the ropes and into position. Secure a loose-fitting zip tie under each rope hole to secure the board in place. (The zip ties should be tight enough to hold the board in place, yet still loose enough to slide up and down the rope to make any necessary adjust-

ments.) Once you get the right placement and the board is level, tighten the zip ties and add two to three more to ensure that the boards won't slide under the weight of the potted plants. Trim away any excess using the diagonal pliers. Repeat these steps with the remaining four boards.

10: Place the plants

Put your potted plants in the holes, step back, admire, and enjoy!

What can go wrong?

The boards are uneven.

Getting the boards level is the most time-consuming and difficult part. It's trial and error; just keep adjusting them until they're level.

Water drips on the floor.

Use wire to attach small glass bottles underneath the bottom row of plants to catch any water that drains through the pots.

Alternatives

If a whole wall seems too ambitious, make a single shelf supported by brackets. You can vary the size of the rope or even the color of the rope and change the color of the pots by painting them. The sky's the limit when it comes to color combinations.

What if you don't want it anymore?

If you get tired of indoor gardening, you can always install it outside.

HOME OFFICE

Flip Desk

With the flip desk, I set out to create a small, simple desk designed for multi-tasking. It's tailor-made for the small apartment or office where space and storage are at a premium. More than just a workstation, the desk can double as a craft table, a dinner table for one, a make-up station or vanity, or a place to store mail. Use it as a workspace during the day and tuck everything out of sight in the evening.

Estimated Time:
6 hours

Estimated Cost:
Under $150

Supplies:
1 4' × 8' sheet of ¾"-thick PureBond birch-veneer plywood
1¼" wood screws
4 1½" cabinet hinges with screws
1¼" stainless steel finish screws
4 28"-high iron hairpin table legs
¾" wood screws
1 2×3 of scrap wood (optional)
Chalkboard paint (optional)
Small mirror (optional)
Double-sided tape (optional)

Tools:
Ruler
Pencil
Circular saw with plywood blade
Clamps
Cordless drill with driving bit
Hammer and chisel
Orbital sander
100- and 220-grit sandpaper
Clean rag
Paintbrush

NOTES: I used PureBond birch-veneer plywood, but any ¾-inch-thick plywood will work. There are a lot of different veneer options, and this desk could look really cool with any of them.

If you're using a circular saw with a laser guide, affixing a guide fence isn't needed because you can just follow the pencil lines.

You don't have to use hairpin legs for this project; almost any premade table or desk legs will work.

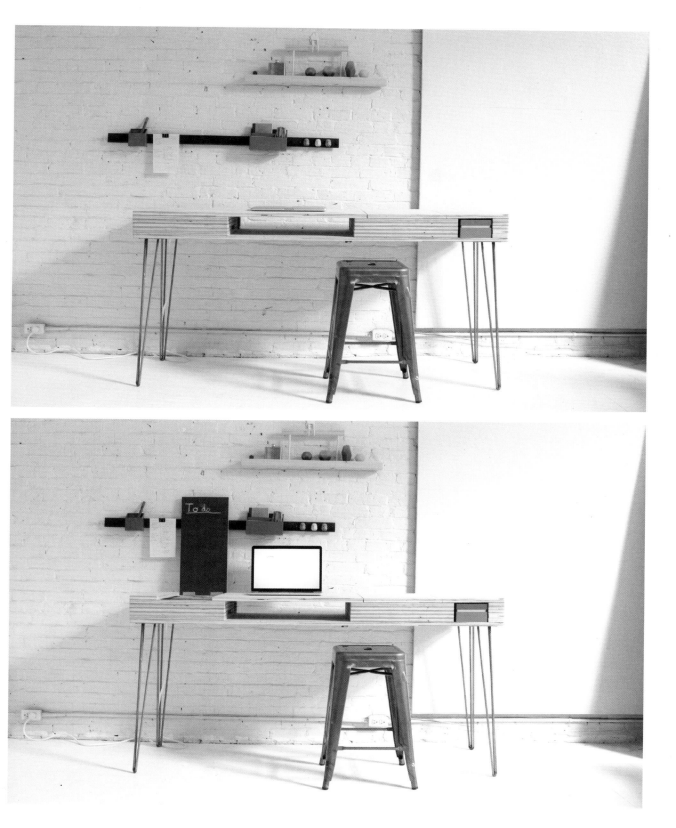

1: Cut the plywood sheet

Follow the diagram to measure, mark, and cut the plywood sheet; note some cuts are best made by your local home improvement store. Be sure to clamp the plywood to your worktable prior to cutting, and use the plywood blade to reduce the amount of tear out for each cut. Set the top and bottom pieces aside.

2: Cut the plywood strips

Measure, mark, and cut the 6" × 5'6" piece into two 3" × 5'6" pieces using the ruler, pencil, and circular saw. From the 2'6" × 4' piece of plywood, measure, mark, and cut twenty-four 2" strips using the ruler, pencil, and circular saw.

3: Cut the strips to length

Measure and mark the strips (cut in step 2) to size using the ruler and pencil. These strips will be stacked five high to create the compartments in the desk. Cut the pieces for the front side of the desk first because you'll have just enough plywood to make the desk. (Some small, stacked pieces used on the interior walls will have gaps.) Using the circular saw, cut five pieces 1" to 9" long from the 3" strips. From the 2" strips, cut the 1'5"-long pieces and the 1'6"-long pieces.

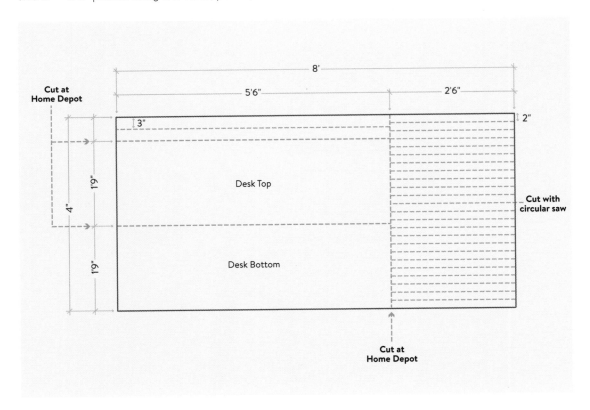

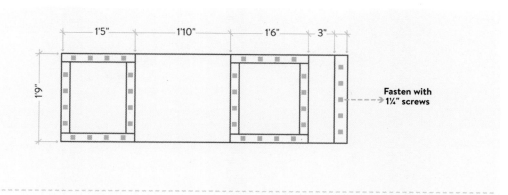

Fasten with
1¼" screws

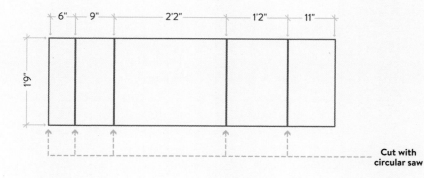

Cut with
circular saw

4: Screw the strips to the bottom

Lay the bottom piece of the desk right side up on your work surface. Follow the diagram to stack and screw the plywood strips together, one at a time, using the cordless drill and 1¼" screws. You'll need to vary the locations of the screws to avoid bumping into the screws on the lower layers of plywood. Set this aside.

5: Mark and cut the desktop

Lay the top piece of the desk horizontally and right side up on your work surface. Working from left to right, follow the diagram to measure and mark four vertical lines at 6", 15", 41", and 55" using the ruler and pencil. Clamp the wood to your worktable and use the circular saw to cut along these lines, making sure to keep them in their original order. You should have five pieces: one 6" wide, one 9" wide, one 2'2" wide, one 1'2" wide, and one 11" wide. Cutting the desktop like this will allow different sections to flip up when hinges are added.

6: Screw the hinges to the desktop sections

Attach two hinges to the undersides of both the 9"-wide section and the 1'2"-wide section using the cordless drill and the screws that come packaged with the hinges.

7: Mark the hinge locations

Lay the bottom piece of the desk that you set aside in step 4 right side up on your work surface. Position the five desktop sections in order and on top. For the two sections with hinges, mark the outline of the hinges on the top layer of stacked plywood at the back of the desk using the pencil. Remove all the sections and set them aside.

8: Cut recesses for the hinges

To make the recessed areas, use the circular saw with the blade set at ⅛" deep to cut a series of grooves, no wider than the hinge, in the top layer of stacked plywood at the back of the desk. This will allow the hinges to sit flush. Then use the hammer and chisel to remove the leftover wood.

9: Screw the hinged desktop sections into place

Place the two hinged sections back into position on the desk. Screw the remaining halves of the hinges to the desk to affix them. You may not get it perfect the first time, so use two screws at first and test how well it opens and closes to make sure it's properly aligned.

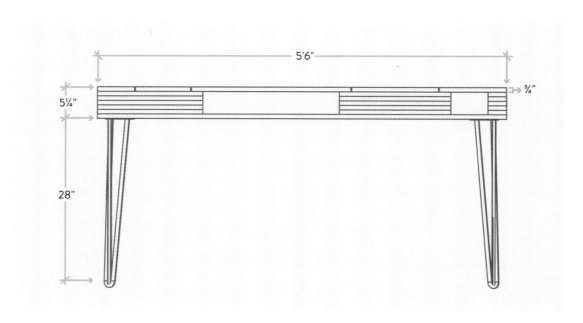

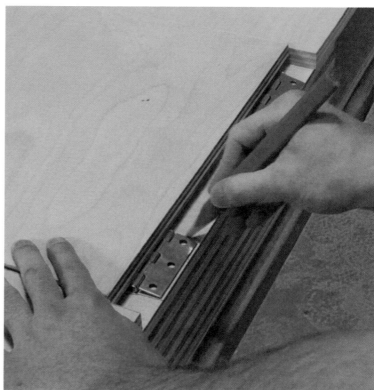

10: Screw on the remaining desktop sections

Position the remaining desktop sections and secure them in place using the cordless drill and the 1¼" stainless steel screws. (They're more expensive than the average deck screw but look much nicer.) You might want to mark the screw locations first to make sure you have uniform placement.

11: Sanding

Lightly sand the top using the orbital sander and 220-grit sandpaper. Sand the sides of the desk using the orbital sander and 100-grit sandpaper followed by the 220-grit sandpaper. Remove the dust using the clean rag.

12: Screw on the legs

Gently flip the desk over and attach the hairpin legs using the cordless drill and ¾" screws. (These shorter screws are used to ensure that they go through only one layer of plywood.)

13: Get organized

You can make interior partitions out of leftover 2×3 scraps and paint stirring sticks, or you can choose to leave the cabinets open. To make the partitions, clamp together two 2×3s and cut grooves into them using the circular saw. The paint sticks fit into the grooves. You can also drill some holes in the 2×3s for some handy cylindrical compartments.

14: Finish

Paint the inside of one flip-up desktop section with chalkboard paint and attach a mirror with double-stick tape to the other.

What can go wrong?

Your cuts are crooked.

If your cuts are crooked or not at perfect right angles, your desk will have a more dramatic texture. You can adjust the roughness with some sanding once the desk is assembled, but the rough, layered texture is the reason many people like this project!

There are gaps in between the plywood layers.

Gaps can occur when the screw pushes up the top layer of wood when securing it. To prevent this, firmly hold the plywood down against the layer below while screwing.

Alternatives

I envisioned this desk as a combination home office and vanity, but it can easily work for a variety of different uses. To make it more home office ready, drill a hole through the desktop to run laptop power cables.

What if you don't want it anymore?

The nice thing about screwing the layers together instead of gluing them is that you can always unscrew and rearrange them to create different sized compartments and shelves. And if you are sick of the look, you can use the plywood pieces to make handy little storage boxes.

Angle Iron Desk

This rustic modern desk is as sturdy as they come. The industrial piece has a versatile look that works equally well in a modern loft or a wood-paneled office. It's made from solid, heavy-duty materials—angle irons and solid 2×10s—and is held together with iron nails, giving it a feel of authenticity and gravitas.

Estimated Time:
5 hours

Estimated Cost:
Under $125

Supplies:
3 8'-long 2×10s
6 36" × 2⅛" angle irons
Lubricating oil for drilling
5 8'-long 2×3s
2½" wood screws
Common nails with a flat broad head
Danish oil

Tools:
Ruler
Pencil
Bench-top chop saw or circular saw
⅛"-diameter drill bit for steel (drill bit size can vary; use one that is designed for metal; it should be slightly larger in diameter than the nails)
Drill press
Clamps
Orbital sander
220-grit sandpaper
Knife or chisel
Tack cloth
Cordless drill with driving bit
Hammer
Cloth rag

NOTE: If you don't have the bench-top tools I used to make this project, you can still make it using hand tools. Instead of the drill press and compound miter saw, you can use a cordless drill, circular saw, speed square, and clamps. To ensure square cuts, clamp the speed square to the wood first to guide the saw.

1: Cut the 2×10s

I cut the 2×10s to length with a compound miter saw. A circular saw guided by a speed square will also work.

2: Cut grooves in desk top boards

In order for the middle angle irons to fit flush, I had to cut grooves into two of the desk top boards. I lined up the two boards that I selected for the outside pieces of the desk top and

clamped them together. I then used one of the shelf boards to mark the location of the grooves. I set my circular saw blade depth to 1¾" and then cut both grooves at the same time. I tested the fit with the angle iron before unclamping the boards.

3: Mark the location of the holes

Using a pencil, mark all six angle irons to indicate the placement of the shelves. I spaced each shelf 7½" apart. Then mark an "X" each place you'll need to drill a hole on the angle irons. For each shelf, mark a single hole that will align with

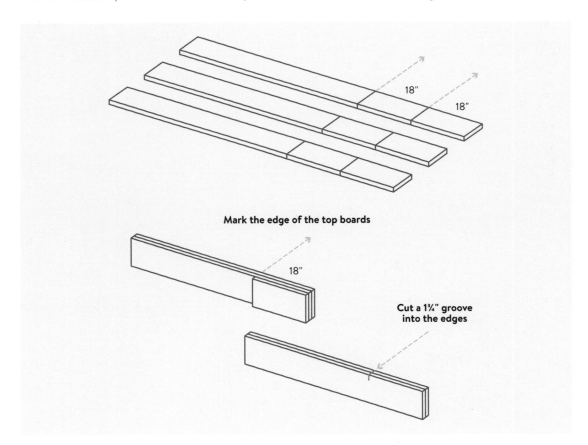

Mark the edge of the top boards

18"

18"

18"

Cut a 1¾" groove into the edges

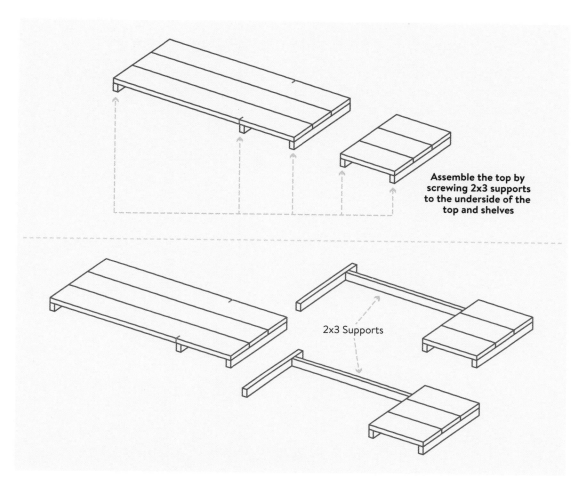

Assemble the top by screwing 2x3 supports to the underside of the top and shelves

2x3 Supports

the long side of the shelf. Then mark two holes, one on top of the other, which will align with the short side of the shelf. The top mark will be for the shelf and the bottom for the 2×3s.

4: Drill through the angle irons

Drilling through steel is different than drilling through wood. Use only the drill bit specifically meant for steel, and check your drill for the appropriate speed settings. Firmly clamp and secure one angle iron to your work surface. Add lubricating oil to the drilling location before you begin. Drill holes through each "X" marked on the angle irons using the drill press and the bit.

5: Cut the 2×3s into supports

Using the circular saw or miter saw, cut the 2×3s into supports equal in length to the width of the 2×10s.

6: Sand the 2×10s

Use the orbital sander and 220-grit sandpaper to sand the supports and the 2×10s. Additionally, the inside corners of the angle irons are not perfectly square and have a slight radius. Round the corners of each 2×10 using a knife or chisel so that they fit into the angle irons. Remove the dust using the tack cloth.

7: Screw the supports onto the shelves

Lay one shelf wrong side up. Place one baluster support on top at each short end. Use 2" screws and the cordless drill to secure them to the shelves. Repeat these steps to add two supports to each remaining shelf.

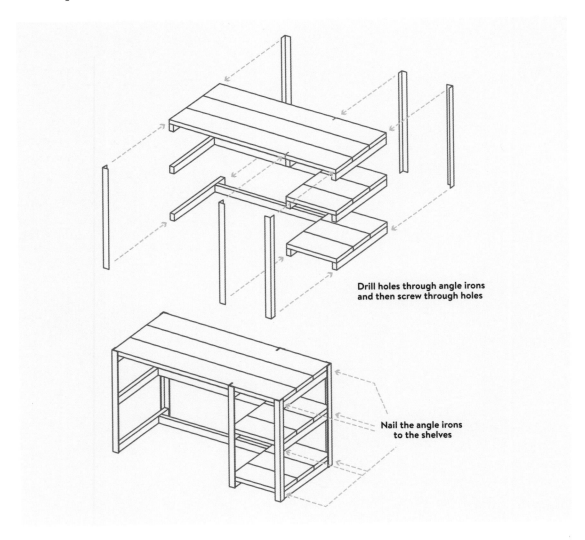

Drill holes through angle irons and then screw through holes

Nail the angle irons to the shelves

8: Nail the back angle irons to the shelves

Lay the three back angle irons on the floor. Position the bottom shelf and drive nails through the angle irons and into both sides of the shelf using the hammer. Next, position the top of the desk. Be sure it's flush with the top of the angle irons before securing it with nails. Now secure the middle shelf.

9: Nail the front angle irons to the shelves

Place one front angle iron on the shelves and make sure it's properly aligned. Beginning at the bottom shelf, drive nails through the angle iron and into the short end of the shelf using the hammer. Position the remaining angle iron at the opposite end and repeat these steps to secure it. Next, align the top shelf and secure it with nails. You may need to use a clamp or a second set of hands to wrestle the wood into place. Secure the two middle shelves, then stand the whole thing up.

10: Drive the nails

Drive nails through the remaining open holes to secure the shelves.

11: Finish the wood

Use a cloth rag to rub a coat of Danish oil into the wood to finish the piece.

What can go wrong?

Warped wood.
2×10s are affordable and look great, but they can be warped, creating a desk that's sturdy and functional but not perfectly square. The angle irons will straighten the desk out slightly, but try not to worry—once it's filled with papers, a laptop, and other items, no one will ever notice that it isn't completely square.

Alternatives

You can change the look of the desk by painting or staining the top. You can also take the angle irons to your local automotive shop and have them powder-coated in a different color.

What if you don't want it anymore?

Disassemble it and turn it into a wood and iron bookcase.

Plywood 3-D Printed Desk

This lightweight, super-modern desk mixes affordable, readily-available materials like EMT conduit and plywood with specialty 3-D printed components. You're going to get a lot of furniture for a relatively small amount of printing. The printed brackets hold the EMT conduit to form trestles that serve both as the legs and a shelf system for the desk. If you like the geometric shape of the desk but don't want to track down a 3-D printer, simply add any ready-made legs you choose.

Estimated Time:
4 hours plus printing time

Estimated Cost:
Under $100

Supplies:
3-D printed brackets set (digital file available on HomeMade-Modern.com)
4 10' × ½" EMT conduit
¾" sheet metal screws or construction adhesive
1 4' × 8' sheet of ¾"-thick plywood
Acrylic clear coat

Tools:
3-D printer
Tube cutter
Vice-grip pliers
Cordless drill with driving bit
Ruler
Pencil
Circular saw with plywood blade
Orbital sander
220-grit sandpaper
Clean rag
Paintbrush

1: Print the brackets

Print the brackets set using the free pattern files available on HomeMade-Modern.com using a 3-D printer. I used an early generation Maker-Bot but you can use any 3-D printer, even the ones found at Kinkos.

2: Cut the conduit

To cut the conduit into the lengths shown in the diagram, tighten the tube cutter around the conduit and use the pliers to grip it. Twist the cutter to create a score line. After a few rotations, tighten the cutter and repeat. Make multiple turns, cutting deeper each time. Once you have a deep score line all the way around, cleanly break off the conduit with your hands. (If you don't have a tube cutter, a hacksaw or the metal-cutting blade on the Ryobi JobPlus with Multi-Tool Attachment will also work.)

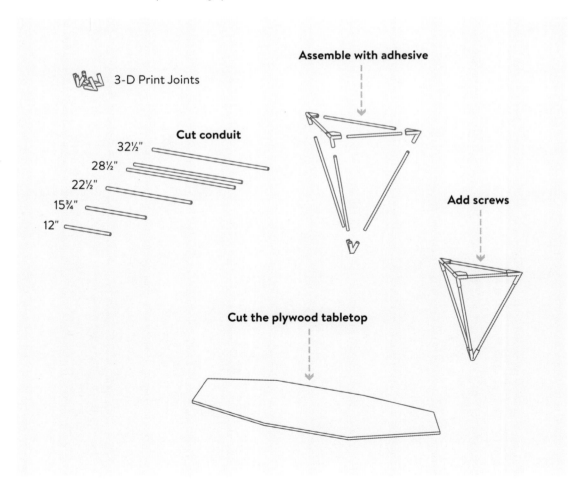

3-D Print Joints

Cut conduit

32½"

28½"

22½"

15¾"

12"

Assemble with adhesive

Add screws

Cut the plywood tabletop

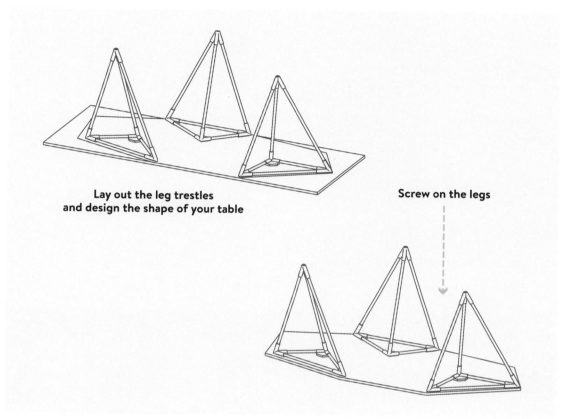

**Lay out the leg trestles
and design the shape of your table**

Screw on the legs

3: Assemble the trestles
Follow the diagram to attach the brackets to the conduit using the cordless drill and ¾" screws and the construction adhesive.

4: Cut the plywood
Measure, mark, and cut the plywood using the ruler, pencil, and circular saw. I like the idea of an irregular geometric design, so I laid out a few lines and made a few cuts with my circular saw.

I used a single layer of plywood since the desk is on the small side. If you want a bigger desk, double up on the plywood along the edges as seen in the Simple Plywood Table (see page 80).

5: Attach the trestles to the desktop
To attach the trestles, screw through the flat parts of the plastic on the brackets and into the plywood using the cordless drill and ¾" screws.

6: Sand and finish

Sand the wood using the orbital sander and 220-grit sandpaper. Use the clean rag to remove the dust. Using the paintbrush, apply one or two coats of the acrylic clear coat according to the manufacturer's instructions. Let dry.

What can go wrong?

The desk wobbles.

A wobbly desk could be caused by the conduit not being securely glued into the sockets. If this is the case, squeeze in some more construction adhesive and consider adding a screw through the outside of the socket and into the conduit. (Be sure to pre-drill a hole before adding a stabilizing screw.)

Alternatives

I added a tower on top to hold a lamp. If you like the shape of the table but don't want to bother with 3-D printing, simply attach some ready-made legs—like hairpin legs.

What if you don't want it anymore?

Simply disassemble it and reuse the components for other projects.

 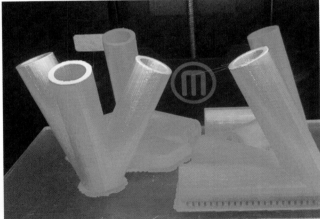

Upgraded Pegboard

Pegboard is composite hardboard that's pre-drilled with evenly spaced holes. Popularized in the 1950s, it's a practical way to store and organize everything from tools to crafts to kitchen items. (Julia Child's famous kitchen pegboard is in the Smithsonian!) We're going to make our own more substantial version with ¾" plywood and bigger holes to accommodate hooks large enough to hang clothing and other objects.

Estimated Time:
4 hours

Estimated Cost:
Under $50

Supplies:
1 4' × 8' sheet of ¾"-thick plywood
1¼" wood screws
¾" diameter dowels (I used four)
Wood scraps (optional)

Tools:
Ruler
Pencil
Circular saw with plywood blade
Cordless drill with driving bit
¾"-diameter drill bit
220-grit sandpaper
Knife

1: **Cut the plywood**

Measure, mark, and cut the plywood sheet using the ruler, pencil, and circular saw, as shown in the diagram. The one pictured was made out of a single sheet of plywood, but if you don't mind using more plywood, it's easier to double up on the plywood instead of cutting a bunch of strips.

2: **Mark the grid**

Lay the largest piece of plywood on your work surface. Leaving a 2" border around all four out-side edges, draw a grid of 4" squares on the plywood using the ruler and pencil.

3: **Attach the back strips**

Flip the plywood over so that the unmarked side is facing up. Position the plywood strips as shown in the diagram. Secure them in place using the cordless drill and 1¼" wood screws. These strips add stability to the pegboard.

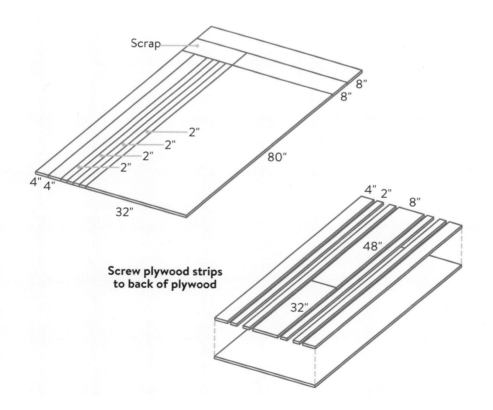

Screw plywood strips
to back of plywood

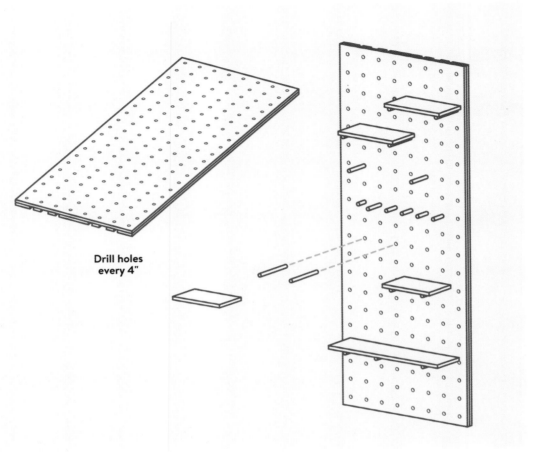

Drill holes every 4"

4: Drill holes

Flip the plywood back over on your work surface. Drill holes where each drawn line intersects using the cordless drill and ¾" bit. Drill all the way through both boards of plywood.

5: Make your own accessories

You can make pegs and shelves for your pegboard by cutting lengths of ¾" dowel. These lengths should be 1½" longer than the distance you want them to protrude from the pegboard. For example, if you want a 9" long peg, you should cut a 10½" long piece of dowel. You can use pipe clamps or zip ties to keep shelves from sliding off the dowels.

The holes are too tight or too loose for the pegs.

You can wrap masking tape around the pegs that are too small for the holes and sand down pegs that are too tight.

Paint and stains can be applied to the pegboard to make this organizational system fit almost any style.

Move the piece outdoors or to the garage to use as a storage system for tools.

BEDROOM

Platform Bed

Most of us could use a little more storage in our bedrooms. The pine deck of this platform bed lifts up to reveal plenty of storage space, allowing you to stow away items that can make a room feel cluttered. Even though this project is on a larger scale than the others, don't be intimidated. It's a fairly simple project to make. If you can make right-angled cuts and drive a screw, you can make this bed!

Estimated Time:
6 hours

Estimated Cost:
Under $150

Supplies:
8'-long 2×10s
8'-long 2×6s
3 8'-long 2×4s
2½" wood screws
8"-wide boards of ¾"-thick pine
4"-wide boards of ¾"-thick pine
6"-wide boards of ¾"-thick pine
10"-wide boards of ¾"-thick pine
8 2½" hinges with coordinating screws
Danish oil
Bed slats
Full mattress (about 53" x 74½")

Tools:
Ruler
Pencil
Compound miter saw
Cordless drill with driving bit
Speed square
Circular saw
Hammer and chisel
Orbital sander
220-grit sandpaper
Clean rag

NOTE: Bed slats or a slatted bed base can be purchased from Amazon or Ikea.

1: Cut the 2×10s, 2×6s, and 2×4s

Follow the diagram to measure, mark, and cut the 2×10s, 2×6s, and 2×4s to their appropriate lengths using the ruler, pencil, and compound miter saw.

2: Assemble the base

Follow the diagram to secure the pieces together using the cordless drill and 2½" screws.

3: Cut the pine

Follow the diagram on page 156 to measure, mark, and cut the pine boards using the ruler, pencil, and compound miter saw. Lay out the pieces for the four storage lids.

4: Screw the lids together

Secure the four lids together using the cordless drill and 2½" screws. Use the speed square to double-check and make sure the pieces are square.

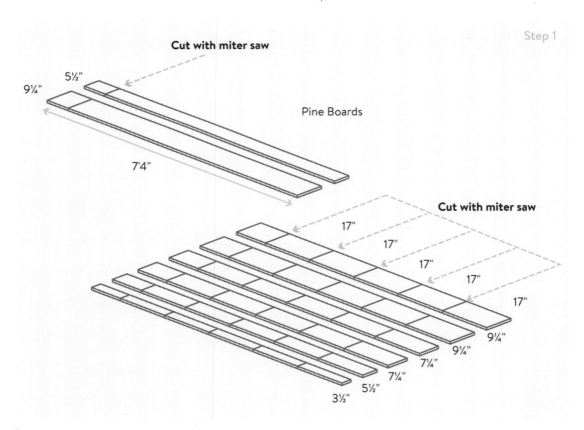

Step 1

Cut with miter saw

5½"

9¼"

Pine Boards

7'4"

Cut with miter saw

17"
17"
17"
17"
17"

9¼"
9¼"
7¼"
7¼"
5½"
3½"

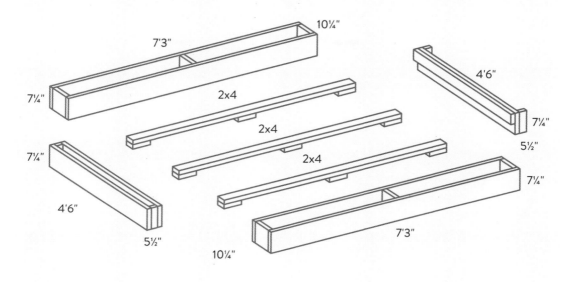

7'3"
10¼"
7¼"
2x4
4'6"
7¼"
7¼"
2x4
5½"
2x4
7¼"
4'6"
5½"
10¼"
7'3"

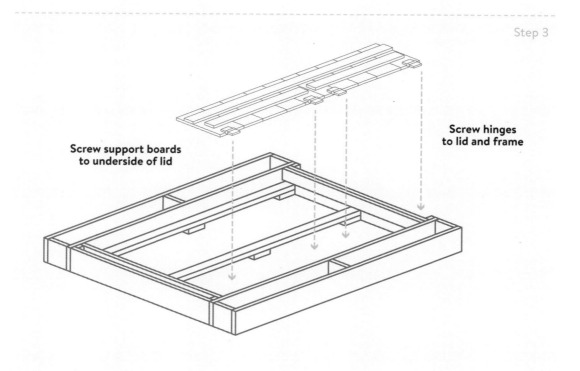

Screw support boards to underside of lid

Screw hinges to lid and frame

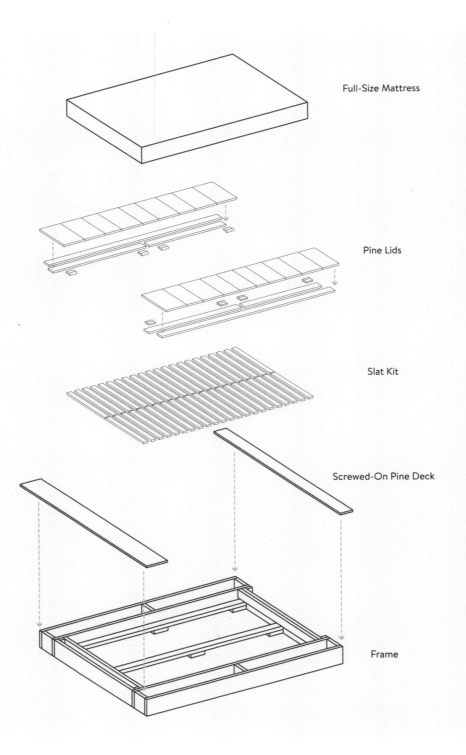

Full-Size Mattress

Pine Lids

Slat Kit

Screwed-On Pine Deck

Frame

5: Screw on pine deck

Place the wider pine deck board at the base of the bed frame and screw it into place. Then place the lids you just assembled on the frame. Then locate and screw the second deck piece onto the frame at the head of the bed.

6: Install the hinges

Using the cordless drill and the screws that come packaged with the hinges, secure the hinges to the lid with the screws they came with. Place the lid on the base and use the pencil to mark the locations where the hinges meet the 2×10s. You'll need to cut recesses into the 2×10s in these spots so that the hinges can sit flat. Use the circular saw with the blade set at ⅛" to cut a series of grooves to make the recessed areas. Then use the hammer and chisel to remove the leftover wood. Screw the remaining halves of the hinges to the base and check to make sure the lid opens correctly.

7: Sand and finish

Sand the wood using the orbital sander and 220-grit sandpaper. Since pine is a softwood, you can also hand sand it pretty quickly if you don't have an orbital sander. Use the clean rag to remove the dust. Then use it to apply one or two coats of the Danish oil according to the manufacturer's instructions. Let dry.

8: Make the bed

Position the slats and place the mattress on top.

What can go wrong?

The lids are crooked.

Installing hinges can be tricky, and you might not get it right the first time. If the lids are opening crooked, just unscrew them and reinstall. It's helpful to have a second set of hands when attaching the lids. Just be patient and take your time.

Alternatives

Add a headboard! Some people love the look of a headboard, and it isn't hard to make an attractive one using only a few pine boards either attached to the bed frame or to the wall itself.

What if you don't want it anymore?

Disassemble the bed and reuse the components. Because you'll end up with relatively large wood pieces, you can reuse the materials for almost any project. The pine boards can be used for shelves or the Herb Garden Wall (see page 118), and the construction lumber can be used for pipe tables or benches.

Garment Rack Closet Solution

Who couldn't use a little more clothes storage space? The great thing about this storage rack is that it actually functions as a way to display some of your favorite clothes. Have a particularly attractive collection of shirts or ties? This is a great way to highlight those favorite items. Another option is to use the garment rack as a wardrobe-staging zone. Streamline your weekday mornings by getting your work wardrobe organized for the entire week.

Estimated Time:
4 hours

Estimated Cost:
Under $90

Supplies:
2 10' × ½" EMT conduit
2 18"-long 2×3 scraps for cross supports
2 18" × 48" pieces of ¾"-thick laminated pine board
1 8'-long 2×8
2 ½" wood screws
2 ½"-diameter EMT inside corner pull elbows
2 48"-long wooden dowels with a 1¼" diameter
1½" wood screws
3" wood screws
2 sets of skateboard wheels
¾" wood screws
Cup hooks (optional)

Tools:
Tube cutter
Vise-grip pliers or locking pliers
Ruler
Painter's tape
½" conduit bender
Pencil
Circular saw
Flathead screwdriver
Cordless drill with driving bit
¾"-diameter drill bit
Orbital sander
220-grit sandpaper
Clean rag
¹⁄₁₆"-diameter drill bit

NOTES: Home Depot sells pre-cut, laminated pine boards with perfectly square corners that are easy to work with. You can make a larger garment rack for less money by switching to plywood, but I like the convenience of these pre-cut boards.

If you can only find a 10-foot-long 2×8 (instead of an 8-foot-long 2×8), simply have the nice people at your local home improvement store cut them down for you.

I used skateboard wheels that I bought online, but simple casters from a home improvement store would work as a cheaper alternative.

1: Cut the conduit

To cut the conduit into four 5' lengths, tighten the tube cutter around the conduit and use the pliers to grip it. Twist the cutter to create a score line. After a few rotations, tighten the cutter and repeat. Make multiple turns, cutting deeper each time. Once you have a deep score line all the way around, cleanly break off the conduit with your hands. (If you don't have a tube cutter, a hacksaw or the metal-cutting blade on the Ryobi JobPlus with Multi-Tool Attachment will also work.)

2: Measure, mark, and bend the conduit

On one 5' length of conduit, measure and mark 11" from one end using the ruler and painter's tape. This is where you'll bend the conduit. Measure and mark the remaining three lengths in the same way. Use the conduit bender to make a 45-degree bend in all four lengths at the taped marks. (If you don't have a conduit bender you can try putting the conduit between two boards to bend it.)

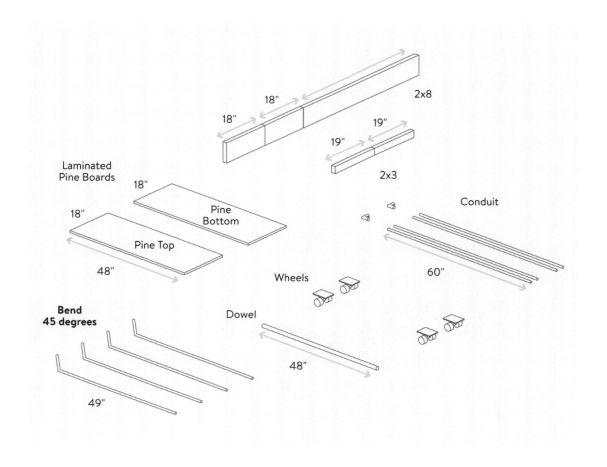

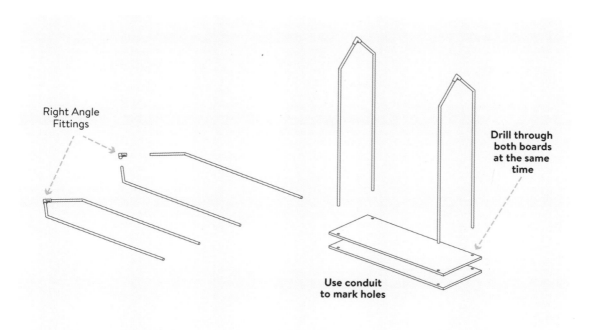

Right Angle Fittings

Drill through both boards at the same time

Use conduit to mark holes

3: Cut the cross supports

Using the ruler, pencil, and circular saw, measure, mark, and cut two 18"-long pieces from the scrap 2×3s to make cross supports that are the same width as the pine boards.

4: Cut the sides and back of the base

The laminated pine boards are the top and bottom of the wood base. To cut the sides and back, measure, mark, and cut two 18"-long pieces for the side, and one field-measured piece for the middle support from the 2×8 using the ruler, pencil, and circular saw.

5: Mark hole locations

Temporarily use one inside corner pull elbow and the flathead screwdriver to secure two lengths of conduit together. Position this structure perpendicular to one short end of one laminated pine board. Use the pencil to trace around the conduit ends to mark the hole locations on the pine board. Repeat these steps to mark the hole locations on the opposite short end.

6: Drill the holes

Drill the holes through both laminated pine boards at the same time using the cordless drill and the ¾" bit.

7: Drill more holes

Use the conduit structure from step 4 to mark the hole locations on the two 18"-long cross supports from step 3 and the two dowels. Drill holes through the cross supports and the dowels using the cordless drill and the ¾" bit.

8: Sand the pieces

Use the orbital sander and 220-grit sandpaper to smooth the edges on all the wood pieces for the base, the cross supports, and dowels. Remove the dust with the clean rag.

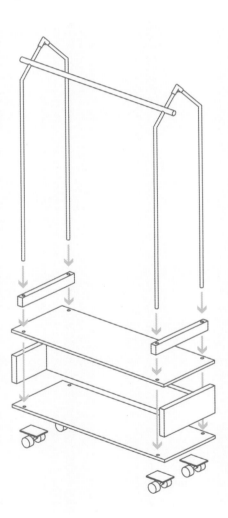

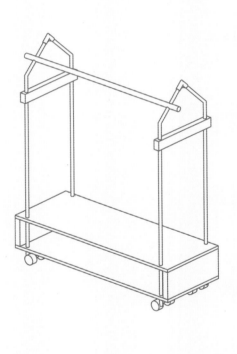

9: Assemble the base

Assemble the base using the cordless drill and the 1½" screws and the 3" screws.

10: Add wheels to the base

Turn the base wrong side up. To keep the conduit from sliding through the base, secure the skateboard wheels over the holes using the cordless drill and ¾" screws. Turn the base right side up.

11: Assemble the rack

Unscrew and remove the inside corner pull elbow from the two 5' length of conduit you secured together in step 5. Insert one length of conduit into each hole in the base. Thread on one cross support on each end of the conduit from the bottom. Then add the dowels as shown or as desired. If the conduit pieces do not slide smoothly, use the drill to make the holes slightly larger. Secure two lengths of conduit together using one inside corner pull elbow and the flat-head screwdriver. Repeat to secure the remaining two lengths of conduit.

12: Fasten the dowels

Once you get the dowels in the desired position, drill a pilot hole through both sides of the dowel and into the metal conduit using the cordless drill and ¾" bit. Then use a single ¾" screw in each hole to fix the dowel into position. Repeat these steps to secure the opposite side of the same dowel and the remaining dowel. Use this same method and additional ¾" screws to fix the cross supports in place too.

13: Add hooks

For the final touch, add cup hooks or pegs to the outsides of the cross supports.

What can go wrong?

The conduit doesn't fit.

Bending the conduit too far or in the wrong place makes it hard to assemble the rack. You can try re-bending it by hand, but since conduit is so inexpensive, I recommend cutting and bending a new piece. Another issue could arise if you didn't drill the cross supports perfectly straight. Simply use a ⅞"-diameter drill bit to create a slightly larger hole to make this less of an issue.

Alternatives

Paint the conduit first with a primer and then spray paint to add some color and a more refined look.

What if you don't want it anymore?

Take it apart and use the skateboard wheels for any other project that you want to add mobility to. The pine boards can be used to make a night stand or a small table/desk.

Pine Night Stand

This night stand in the mid-century modern style is made from ¾" pine boards. It's inexpensive and easy to work with, and the wood is soft, which makes cutting, screwing, and sanding satisfying and nearly effortless.

Estimated Time:

2 hours

Estimated Cost:

Under $25

Supplies:

1 10" × 8' piece of ¾"-thick pine board
1 8'-long 2×3
2 48"-long wooden dowels with a 1" diameter
Interior house paint in a semi-gloss finish with a low VOC (optional)
1½" screws
Wood glue

Tools:

Ruler
Pencil
Circular saw
Clamps
Cordless drill with driving bit
1"-diameter drill bit
¹⁄₁₆"-diameter drill bit for pilot holes
Orbital sander
220-grit sandpaper
Clean rag
Paintbrush (optional)

1: Cut the wood with the circular saw

Measure, mark, and cut the 10"×8' pine board, the 6"×8' pine board, and the 2×3 into the lengths shown in the diagram using the ruler, pencil, and circular saw.

2: Drill the holes

Stack up all the pine boards and clamp them to your work surface. Drill through both the pine boards and the pieces of 2×3 at the same time using the cordless drill and 1" bit. It's helpful if you put a piece of scrap wood underneath the boards to reduce tear out.

3: Sand the 2×3s

Sand the 2×3s using the orbital sander and 220-grit sandpaper. Once you assemble the night stand, it will be difficult to reach them so do it before you put the night stand together. Remove the dust with the clean rag.

4: Paint the 2×3s

Paint the 2×3s using the paintbrush and interior house paint. This step is optional, of course, but if you want to add some color, paint the pieces now before assembling the night stand.

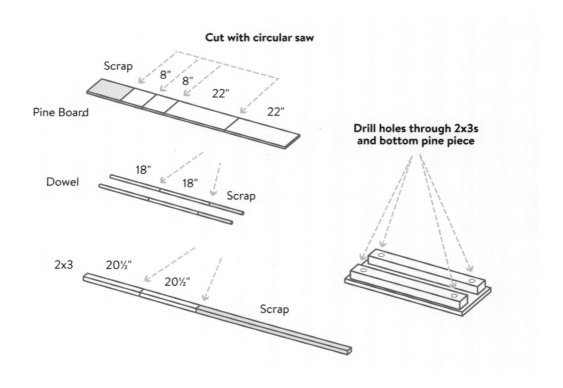

Cut with circular saw

Scrap

8" 8" 22" 22"

Pine Board

Dowel

18" 18" Scrap

2x3 20½" 20½" Scrap

Drill holes through 2x3s and bottom pine piece

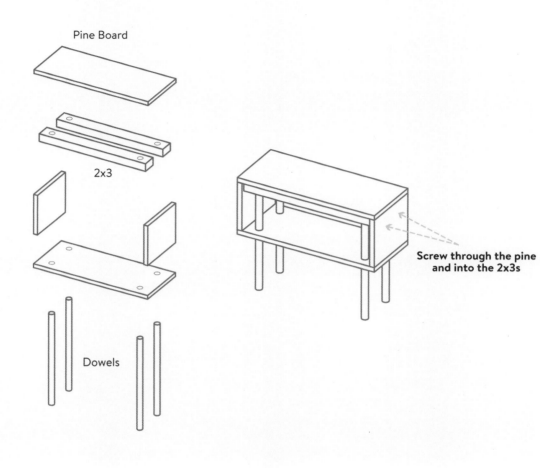

Pine Board

2x3

Dowels

**Screw through the pine
and into the 2x3s**

5: Cut the dowels

Cut four 18"-long pieces of dowels to use as legs.
This will result in a night stand with a top surface that is 18¾" from the floor. You can make
this higher or lower by changing the length of
the legs.

6: Assemble with screws

Follow the diagram to assemble the pieces into
a box using the cordless drill and the 1½" screws.
Make sure that the holes for the dowels align.

7: Glue in the legs and sand

Apply wood glue to the ends of the legs and insert them into the holes. Let dry. Give the piece a final sanding using the orbital sander and 220-grit sandpaper. Remove the dust with the clean rag.

What can go wrong?

You drilled the holes in the wrong place.
Drilling the holes in the wrong place can make it difficult to assemble the night stand or result in legs that are at odd angles. You can always

drill slightly larger holes to make the fit easier, but the result will be wobbly legs. If the legs do wobble, use a hot glue gun or construction adhesive to fill in the extra space between the hole and the dowel.

Alternatives

Try different colors and sizes to make a series of handy end tables and night stands for your home.

What if you don't want it anymore?

Pull the legs off and you have a nice storage crate.

Concrete Night Stand

I had so much fun making this quirky little night stand that looks slightly like a robot. It's the perfect way to express your love for Lego. For this project, I use a Lego forming technique that is also used for the Concrete Nesting Tables (see page 62), but this time we add additional materials to finish the piece. Not only can you achieve incredibly precise joints with Lego-formed concrete, it's also super easy to make.

Estimated Time:
6 hours plus curing time

Estimated Cost:
Less than $40

Supplies:
1 2' × 4' sheet of ¾"-thick melamine board
1×6, 1×8, 2×2, 2×3, 2×4, 2×6, and 2×8 dot Lego bricks (I built the mold 25 layers high. The larger 2×6 and 2×8 bricks are the best for making cross braces.)
1 80-pound bag of commercial-grade Quikrete Countertop Mix or Quikrete 5000 Concrete Mix

Tools:
Hot glue gun and glue sticks
Spoon or small shovel for mixing the concrete
Plastic bowl or mixing tray
Stick or dowel
Knife
Long-nose pliers (optional)

NOTES: I used classic Lego bricks to make the mold. I raided my parents' attic to retrieve my childhood stash and purchased a few new additional sets.

I prefer the smoother look of the Quikrete Countertop Mix for these types of projects, but Quikrete 5000 will work just fine too.

1: Lay out the mold

Lay the sheet of melamine right side up on your work surface. Follow the diagram (see below) to build the Lego mold up three bricks high. Use bricks as temporary spacers between the walls to ensure that the inside and the outside rings are equidistant.

2: Glue down the Lego bricks

Use the hot glue gun to adhere the Lego pieces to the melamine board along the edges. Don't worry—the glue will peel off later.

3: Finish building the mold

Build the mold up brick by brick. When you get to the top, add some support braces (Lego bricks that connect two walls) to keep the walls from bending out under the weight of the concrete.

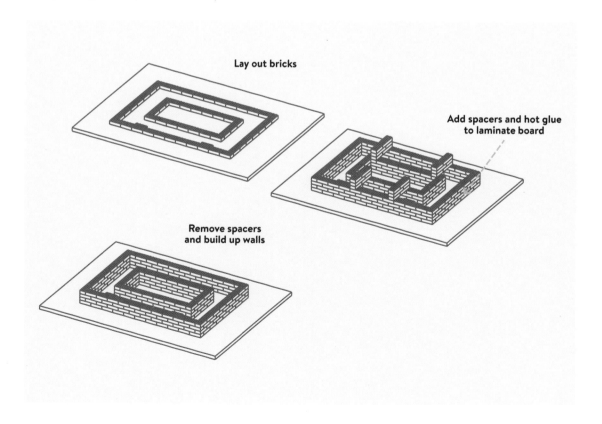

Lay out bricks

Add spacers and hot glue to laminate board

Remove spacers and build up walls

4: Mix and pour the concrete

Mix the concrete and water in a plastic bowl or mixing tray. Different concrete mixes require different amounts of water, so refer to the manufacturer's recommendations for proportions. When it's the consistency of cookie dough, spoon it into the mold. When there is 3" of concrete in the bottom of the mold, use a stick to push the concrete into the corners. This will vibrate the concrete slightly, pushing the air bubbles to the surface. Repeat this process until the mold is full.

5: Level and smooth

If you're enjoying playing with the Lego bricks, make a little Lego trowel to smooth the concrete. A stick or scrap piece of wood will work just as well. Don't worry about smoothing this side completely because the melamine side of the mold is the front, and the concrete will come out perfectly smooth there.

6: Let the concrete cure

Let the concrete cure for at least 20 hours before removing the mold.

7: Remove the mold

Removing the Lego bricks can be a bit time-consuming. Start by removing a few of the top layers. Cut the glue with a knife, then flip the entire piece over to remove additional layers. You can use long-nose pliers to aid in their removal, but be careful not to scratch or bend the bricks.

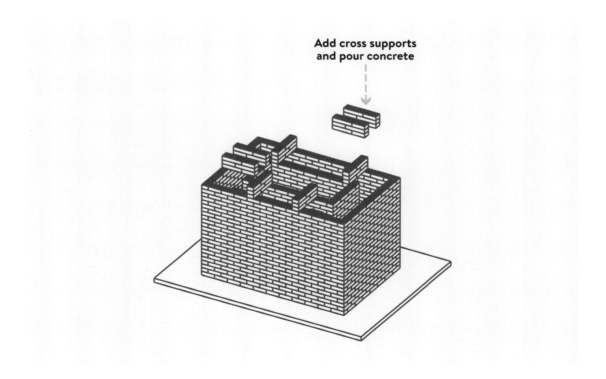

Add cross supports and pour concrete

8: Add a drawer and legs

You can make a base and drawer for this night stand using Lego pieces. The concrete part is quite heavy, so I suggest you glue the Lego bricks together using a hot glue gun. To make the Lego stand and drawer, simply connect bricks together to make tall, wide legs and to make a drawer that fits the opening. I assembled the front face of the drawer and legs with bright green 1×4, 1×2, 1×6, 1×3, 2×2, 2×3, and 2×4 bricks. You can also use larger bricks to make the process a little easier. To make the wooden legs, cut two pieces from a 2×10 and connect them by inserting and gluing a ¾" diameter wood dowel into ¾" holes. To make the drawer, cut pieces from the 2×10 and make a box that fits within the concrete part of the night stand. I drilled two 1" diameter holes to use as handles.

9: Clean the Lego bricks

Most of the dried concrete will flake off the Lego bricks. Any remaining pieces can be scraped or brushed off with a toothbrush. Use cold water and a mild, non-abrasive soap to wash the bricks by hand or place the bricks in a mesh laundry bag and machine-wash them on cold. Do *not* use hot water or you will warp the bricks.

What can go wrong?

The concrete breaks!
Go slow when removing the bricks. Use long-nose pliers and remove the bricks from the bottom if they're stubborn or stuck. Also, let the concrete cure longer in order to increase its strength before you remove the mold. (Concrete does not reach its full strength until it has cured for weeks.)

Alternatives

The Lego-mold method is incredibly versatile. There are so many cool things you can make with this technique, like the Concrete Nesting Tables (see page 62) or even experiment with smaller concrete accessories. I made fantastic concrete planters using this technique.

What if you don't want it anymore?

A great feature of concrete is that it weathers incredibly well, so this piece can easily be moved outside where it can be used as a plant stand.

Vertical Valet

This is a project I developed for my own use, and it works as sort of a mini mudroom storage system. It's a perfect piece of furniture if you live with roommates and need a way to keep yourself organized. It is a station for storing and unloading and is great for holding keys, a cell phone, loose change, hanging a book bag, coats, an umbrella, gloves, mail, and tons of other things. You should adapt this project to your own particular habits by adding or subtracting additional hooks, shelves, and boxes to fit your needs.

Estimated Time:
3 hours

Estimated Cost:
Under $25

Supplies:
1 8" × 8' piece of ¾"-thick pine board
2 8" × 8'-long ¾"-thick pine boards
1 8'-long 2×3
1 48"-long wooden dowel with a ¾" diameter
1½" screws
2½" screws
Coat hooks

Tools:
Ruler
Pencil
Circular saw
Clamps
Cordless drill with driving bit
Orbital sander
220-grit sandpaper
Clean rag
¾"-diameter drill bit
⅛"-diameter drill bit

1: Cut the pieces

Cut the 2×3 as shown in the diagram. Cut four pieces from the pine board as shown in the diagram.

2: Cut slots in the pine board

Stack the top and bottom pieces of pine and mark a location for the 2×3 to go through. I placed the 2×3 through holes toward the left on pieces (e) and (f) and through the center of pieces (l) and (m). Set your circular saw blade to 1½" and make a series of cuts in a row to remove the wood. You can cut both sides at the same time if you clamp them together.

3: Build the boxes

Using the diagram as a guide, assemble the two boxes and use the cordless drill and ½" screws to secure the pieces together. Be sure the holes for the 2×3 are aligned.

4: Sand the 2×3 pole

Sand all pieces smooth using the orbital sander and 220-grit sandpaper. Remove dust with the clean rag.

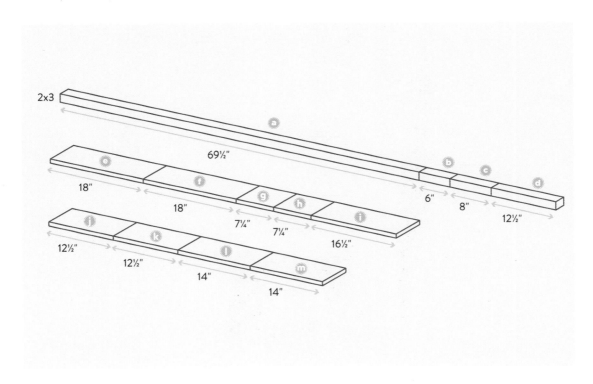

2x3

69½"
18"
18"
7¼"
7¼"
16½"
6"
8"
12½"
12½"
12½"
14"
14"

**Stack boards
and trace 2x3 post**

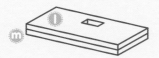

**Drill around perimeter of outline
with ⅛" diameter drill bit**

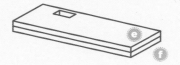

Assemble boxes with screws

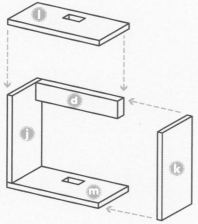

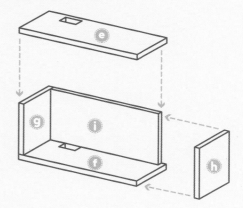

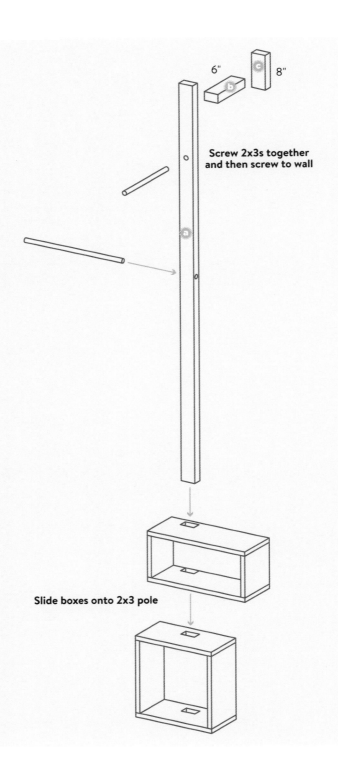

6" 8"

**Screw 2x3s together
and then screw to wall**

Slide boxes onto 2x3 pole

5: Thread on the boxes and shelves

Slide the 2×3 pole through the holes in the boxes.

6: Install

Attach the 6" horizontal arm (b) at the top of the vertical 2×3 pole with 2½" screws and then connect it to piece (c) and the wall. Use a stud finder to locate a stud and then drill diagonally through piece (c) and through the drywall and into the stud using two 2½" screws.

7: Fix the boxes

Now that the vertical pole is attached to the wall, you can slide the boxes into their appropriate positions and secure them using the cordless drill and the 1½" screws.

8: Add pegs

Drill holes for wood dowels, coat hooks, and other hanging accessories using the cordless drill and drill bit. Cut the pegs from the ¾" dowel and insert them in the holes. The dowels should fit in snugly. (I don't like to glue them in if I don't have to so that I can change out the lengths depending on what I want to hang on them.)

What can go wrong?

The valet keeps coming off the wall.

If you are attaching this to drywall I recommend using drywall anchors. Drywall or gypsum board is a weak material that crumbles easily. Drywall anchors create a plastic socket for the screws that result in a stronger connection.

Alternatives

There are an infinite number of ways to implement this concept. I recommend analyzing your own habits and tailoring this project to accommodate the things you use on a regular basis. For example, if you always misplace your keys or work ID tag, have a dedicated hook for those things.

What if you don't want it anymore?

Disassemble, use the pine boxes for storage, or repurpose the 2×3 for the Pipe and Wood Bar Stool (see page 114).

OUTDOORS

Concrete Planter

There's really no better way to warm up your outdoor space than with plants. For this project, I was inspired by those galvanized steel buckets with spigots that are often used outdoors as planters or ice buckets—but I wanted something a bit more industrial and rugged-looking. So when I spotted a beat-up, old kitchen cabinet on a construction site, I grabbed it knowing that it would make the perfect mold for one of my favorite materials—concrete.

Estimated Time:
6 hours plus curing time

Estimated Cost:
Under $60

Supplies:
2"-thick sheets of XPS Rigid Foam Insulation (sizes will depend on the size of the cabinet you salvage)
An old cabinet (see Notes)
Construction adhesive
½" brass pipe (see Notes for length)
Duct tape
Silicone caulk
A ratchet strap, L-brackets, or rope
2 to 3 80-pound bags of Quikrete 5000 Concrete Mix
1 scrap piece of ¾"-thick plywood (equal to the size of the cut foam)
Threaded nut for the pipe
½" spigot
4 metal heavy-duty casters
¾" screws

Tools:
Ruler
Pencil
Circular saw
Cordless drill with driving bit
¾"-diameter drill bit
Knife or box cutter
Concrete mixing tray
Hoe
Shovel
Stick or pipe
Hammer
Circular saw (optional)
Pry bar

NOTES: I salvaged a beat-up, old kitchen cabinet from a construction site. You can scavenge for one at a construction site, a junkyard, or maybe your city has a building reuse center. Use whatever size you'd like.

XPS Rigid Foam is a type of waterproof insulation that is easy to cut. If you don't have a circular saw, use a knife to cut it.

Determine the length of the pipe you need by measuring the depth of your planter wall and then adding a few inches. I used a brass pipe to avoid rust and attached a spigot, but a hose bib could also make the planter easy to drain.

I used all-metal, heavy-duty casters for their strength and their industrial look. Plastic or rubber wheels would be easier on a deck or floors. You could even try using old skateboard wheels.

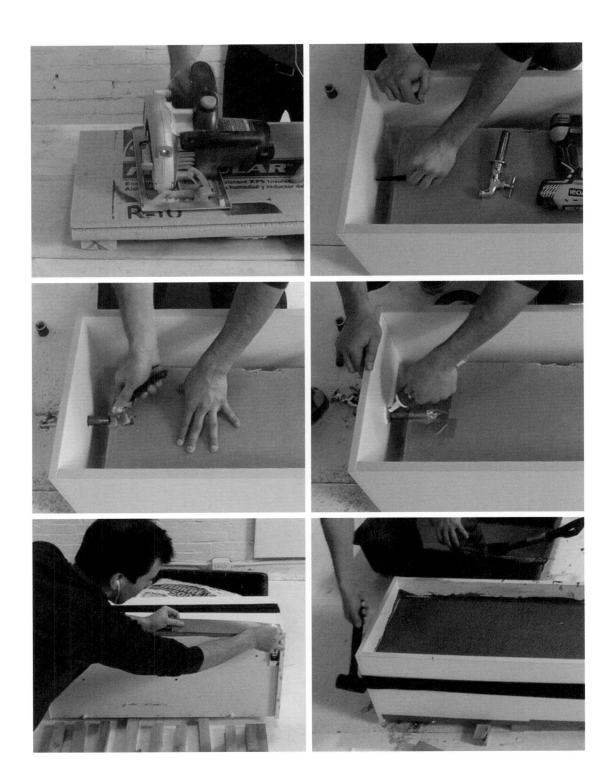

1: Cut the rigid foam

Use the ruler, pencil, and circular saw to measure, mark, and cut three pieces of the rigid foam that are 1½" to 2" smaller on all sides than the size of the base of the cabinet. Center and adhere one piece of foam to the bottom of the cabinet using the construction adhesive. There should be space on all sides between the foam and the four walls of the cabinet. Affix the remaining two pieces on top of the first using the adhesive.

2: Measure and mark where to drill the hole for the spigot

On the inside of the cabinet, measure the distance from the top of the cabinet to the top of the foam. Now measure and mark this same distance on the outside of the cabinet. At this marked spot, drill a hole through the cabinet using the cordless drill and ¾" bit. Insert the pipe into the hole. (I used a hex nut on the end of the pipe to keep the pipe in place. The hex nut will end up on the inside of the cabinet. The pipe threads should stick out from the concrete enough so that you can screw on the spigot, but not so far that the spigot's bib won't be flush with the concrete.)

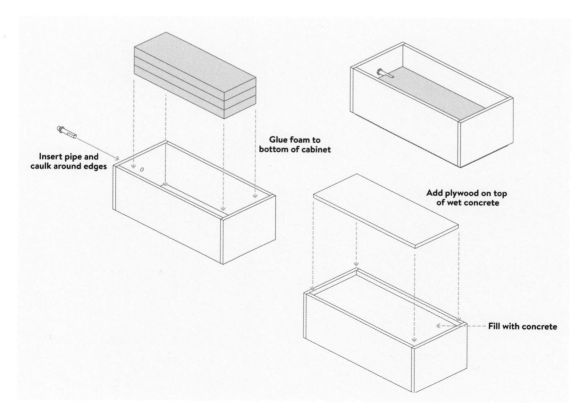

Insert pipe and caulk around edges

Glue foam to bottom of cabinet

Add plywood on top of wet concrete

Fill with concrete

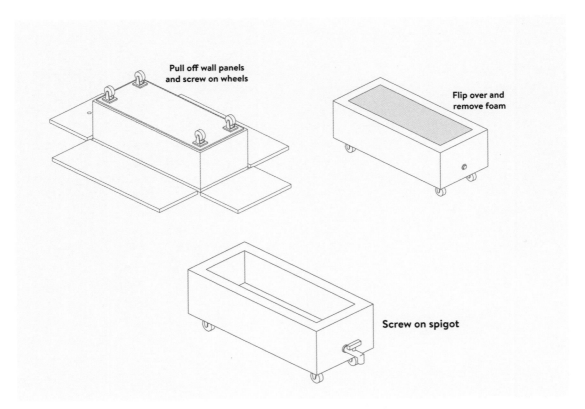

Pull off wall panels and screw on wheels

Flip over and remove foam

Screw on spigot

3: Cut the foam to fit the pipe

Use the knife to cut a trough in the foam to make room for the pipe.

4: Seal the mold

Use duct tape to secure the pipe to the foam. At the hole, use silicone caulk to seal the gaps between the pipe and the cabinet.

5: Brace and mark the mold

It's a good idea to tie something around the cabinet to prevent the weight of the concrete from pushing the cabinet walls apart. I used a ratchet strap, but rope or even L-brackets would also work well. On the inside of the cabinet, mark a line 2" above the top of the foam using the pencil. This will serve as a "fill line" to let you know when you have added enough concrete.

6: Mix and pour the concrete

Mix the concrete and water in a large concrete mixing tray with a hoe. Different concrete mixes require different amounts of water so refer to the manufacturer's recommendations for proportions. (Mixing this much concrete is hard work and you may be tempted to overwater it to make it easier to work with, but adding too much water weakens the concrete and could cause it to crack.) When it's the consistency of cookie dough, shovel it into the mold. Use a stick or pipe to pack the concrete down into all the corners and cracks of the cabinet. Make sure the wet concrete goes under and around the pipe. Fill it with concrete up to your pencil line.

7: Vibrate the mold
Using a hammer, shake and vibrate the mold by tapping the surface of the cabinet. This will bring the air bubbles to the surface of the concrete.

8: Put in the plywood
Cut a scrap piece of plywood equal in size to the rigid foam cut in step 1 using the circular saw. To create a mounting surface for the casters, center the plywood and push it into the wet concrete until it is flush with the surface. You may need to put something heavy on top of it to keep it from floating up.

9: Let the concrete cure
Let the concrete cure for at least four days before removing the mold. You can control the moisture better by covering the concrete as it dries.

10: Remove the outer mold
Gently break away the cabinet mold without cracking the concrete. You can use a circular saw to cut away the cabinet, if needed.

11: Remove the inner mold
Use a knife and pry bar to cut and break out the foam.

12: Install the spigot and screw on the wheels
Screw the spigot on and seal it with caulk. Or you can glue it on with construction adhesive. Then turn the entire piece wrong side up. Attach the casters to the plywood using the cordless drill and ¾" screws. Turn the planter right side up.

What can go wrong?
The concrete cracks.
If you added too much water or tried to take off the mold too soon, the concrete can crack. You can patch the cracks using a concrete adhesive.

Alternatives
If you get tired of gardening you can always use it as an outdoor ice bucket for entertaining.

What if you don't want it anymore?
If you're not able to repurpose this project, you can take it to your nearest concrete recycling center, where it will be ground down into a mix and used as concrete once again.

Geometric Dog House

I couldn't leave man's best friend out in the cold! Despite its faceted, angular, and quite complicated appearance, this modern dog house is quite easy to construct. You can make the entire dog house from a single sheet of plywood, and the design can be scaled up or down to accommodate different sized dogs. If you don't have a pup or a cat, this hollow geometric form also serves as a really stylish laundry basket!

Estimated Time:
6 hours

Estimated Cost:
Under $50

Supplies:
1 4' × 8' sheet of ¼"-thick birch veneer plywood
2 8'-long 2×3s
¾" deck screws

Tools:
Ruler
Pencil
Circular saw with plywood blade
Clamps
200-grit sandpaper
Clean rag
Cordless drill with driving bit

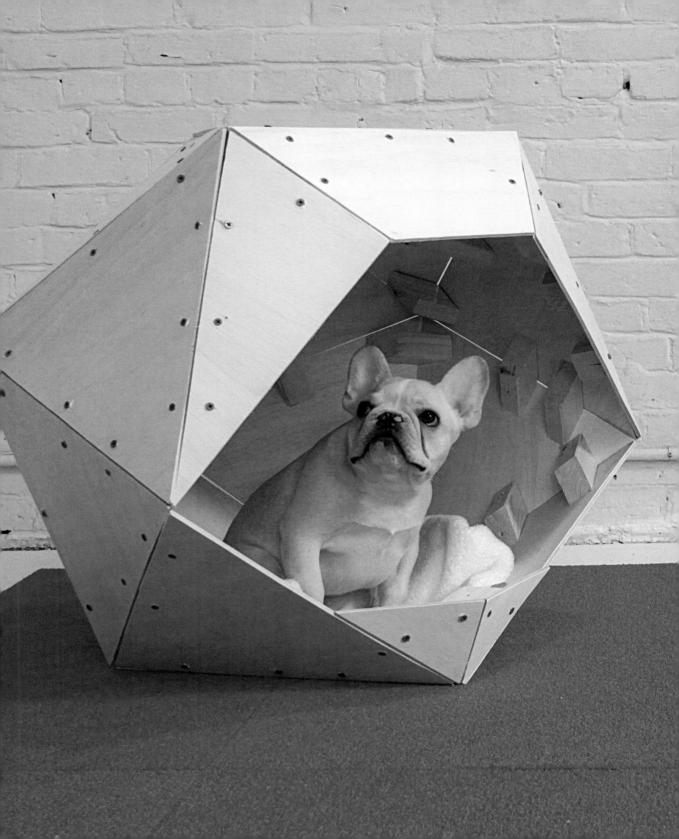

1: Size the dog house

The height of the triangles that make up this dog house should be about the same height as your dog when sitting. When seated, my dog, Fletcher, is about 14" tall. I had my home improvement store measure, mark, and cut two 14" × 8' pieces from the plywood sheet. If you're making a smaller or larger dog house, have the strips cut to the size of your intended triangle.

2: Measure, mark, and clamp the two boards together

The dog house is made up of equilateral triangles. Follow the diagram to measure and mark off the triangles on one 14" × 8' piece of plywood using the ruler and pencil. Place the marked board on top of the remaining 14" × 8' piece of plywood, edges even, and clamp them together. This will allow you to cut the two boards at the same time.

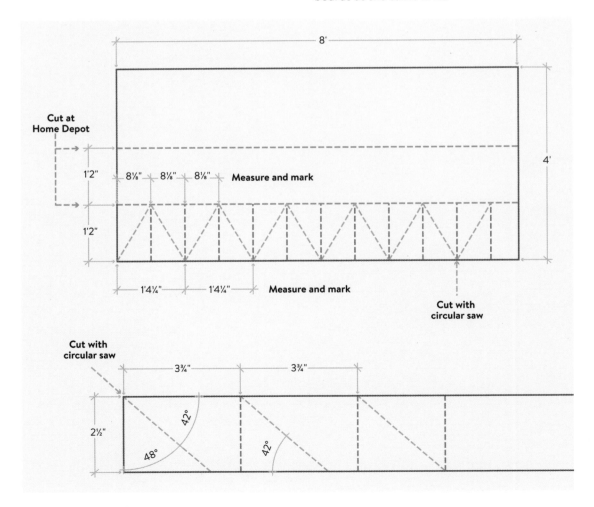

3: Cut the plywood

Once the triangles have been marked, cut along those lines using the circular saw and the laser guide on your circular saw until you have twenty triangles.

4: Measure and cut the angled support blocks

There are two ways to cut the two 2×3s of construction lumber into angled support blocks. If you have a 5½"-diameter circular saw, measure and mark the wood as shown in the diagram on page 190. If you have a 7¼"-diameter or greater circular saw, set the blade to cut at a 42-degree angle to cut the blocks. For this size dog house, cut fifty support blocks using the circular saw.

5: Sand the edges

Use the 200-grit sandpaper to hand sand the edges of all the cut pieces. Remove the dust using a clean rag.

6: Assemble

Position three support blocks, one on each side of one plywood triangle. Secure the plywood to the supports using the cordless drill and ¾" screws. Repeat these steps to join additional plywood triangles as shown.

7: Cut the pieces for the entry

Cut one of the plywood triangles in half and cut the tip of another to make a doorway. Cut some of the plywood triangles down to make the doorway as shown in the photo.

8: Add supports

Add in additional wood blocks on the inside of the house to strengthen the dog house.

What can go wrong?

There are big gaps between the pieces of plywood.

If the brackets are not cut at the correct angle, the plywood pieces will have gaps between them and the entire structure will be misshapen. Take your time in setting up your saw to cut the support blocks at the proper angle. After you cut one, double-check to make sure it's right before cutting the rest of them.

Alternatives

Clean it up and turn it into a stylish laundry basket. I have also used this dog house pattern, scaled down a bit, to make a giant geometric lampshade.

What if you don't want it anymore?

Simply disassemble and use the pieces for other projects.

Concrete Fire Pit

This modern concrete fire pit is a great centerpiece for outdoor entertaining. This isn't a difficult project, but it is time consuming and labor intensive. Concrete fireplaces and fire pits should be constructed carefully. When exposed directly to high amounts of heat, moisture trapped in the concrete can expand and cause the concrete to crack and—in extreme situations—explode. I lined the inside of the fire pit with fire brick and filled the bottom with lava rock to ensure that the majority of the heat didn't come in direct contact with the concrete. If you're building a fire pit in a cold climate, I recommend putting Sonotube footing under each of the four corners to prevent frost heave.

Estimated Time:

16 hours plus curing time

Estimated Cost:

$250

Supplies:

8 2×4s

6 2×6s

2½" deck screws

16 L-brackets

7 50-pound bags of Quikrete All-Purpose Gravel (top size ⅜")

8 ⅜" × 18" pieces of rebar

8 ⅜" × 36" pieces of rebar

8"-, 10"-, 12"-, or 14"-gauge wire

20 to **25** 80-pound bags of Quikrete 5000 Concrete Mix

28 fire bricks

1 bag mortar

2 5-gallon buckets of lava rocks

Tools:

Ruler

Pencil

Circular saw or compound miter saw

Cordless drill with driving bit

Shovel

Level

Large mixing tray or wheelbarrow

Hoe

Steel trowel

Concrete float

1: Make the panels

Use the 2×4s and 2×6s to make the form for the concrete. You're going to be creating two forms—a larger outer ring and a smaller inner ring. Follow the diagram for details on assembling the wood into the panels for the form.

2: Assemble the form

Use the cordless drill, 2½" screws, and L-brackets to assemble the panels, creating your concrete form. You'll end up with two boxes.

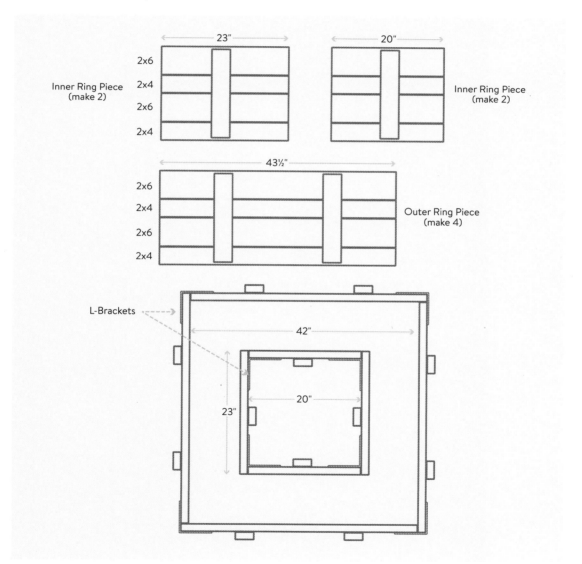

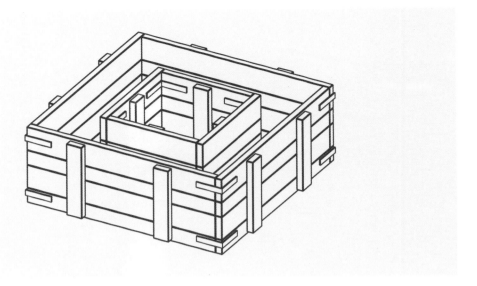

3: Mark the perimeter and dig

Place the frame at the desired location and use the shovel to dig around the frame to mark the perimeter. Then dig about 8" into the ground. Compact the earth and try to make it as level as possible.

4: Prepare to create the foundation

Fill the hole with approximately 3" of gravel and then try to level and compact that gravel. Once the gravel is compacted, place the larger outer ring on the gravel and place the inner ring inside. Check your measurements to be sure that your inner ring is exactly in the center of the larger ring. Once it's perfectly center, secure it in place with the scrap pieces of wood using the cordless drill and 2½" screws. Do one last check with a level to make sure the formwork is per-

fectly level on the ground. Drive two 18"-long pieces of rebar into the ground on each of the sides and then wire in place one 36"-long piece of rebar, horizontally, on each side.

5: Create the fire pit foundation

Mix the concrete and water in a large mixing tray or wheelbarrow using the hoe. Different concrete mixes require different amounts of water, so refer to the manufacturer's recommendations for proportions. (Mixing this much concrete is hard work and you may be tempted to overwater it to make it easier to work with, but adding too much water weakens the concrete and could cause it to crack.) When it's the consistency of cookie dough, add 3" of concrete to the bottom of the form using the shovel. This first concrete pour is the foundation for the entire project, so make sure that you push it down into all the corners. Let the concrete cure for at least 20 hours.

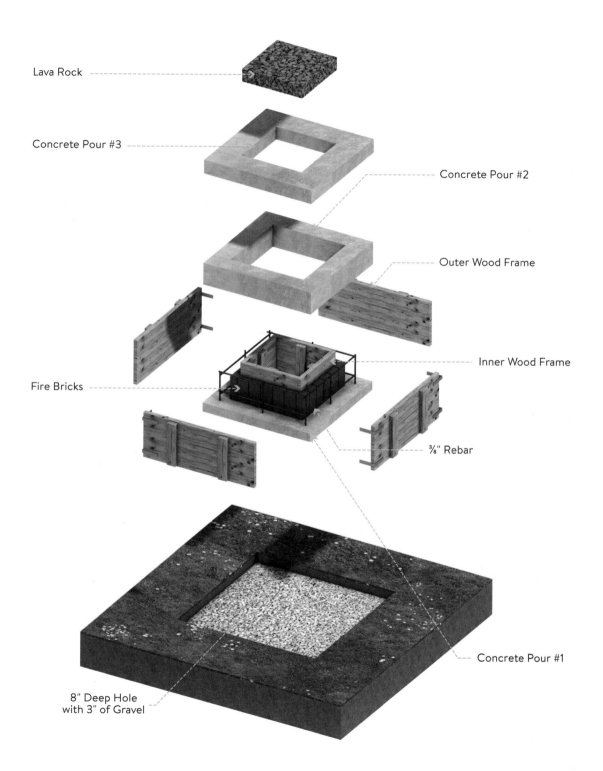

Lava Rock

Concrete Pour #3

Concrete Pour #2

Outer Wood Frame

Inner Wood Frame

Fire Bricks

³⁄₈" Rebar

Concrete Pour #1

8" Deep Hole
with 3" of Gravel

6: Mix the mortar and add bricks

Mix the mortar per the manufacturer's directions. Using the trowel, spread a layer of mortar around the inside of the formwork. Then place each brick, one at a time, vertically, against the inside formwork with mortar between the layers. Don't worry too much about the aesthetics. Your bricks will just get sooty and black after time, and no one will pay attention to your bricklaying skills.

7: Add more concrete

Mix and add an additional 5" of concrete on top of the bricks. Let your concrete cure for an additional 20 hours.

8: Add your final concrete layer

Remove the scrap wood that has been connecting the inner and outer formwork. Mix and add enough concrete to fill the form. Once the formwork is full, use a trowel or straight scrap piece of wood to smooth out the top. Wait 1 hour and then use a float to completely level out the surface of the concrete. Wait an additional hour and then finish smoothing with a steel trowel. Cover the concrete with a tarp to allow it to cure. Make sure that the tarp is not touching the wet concrete. After 48 hours, remove the wooden molds.

9: Create a thermally resistant surface for the fire

Add two 5-gallon buckets of lava rock to the bottom of the fire pit to create the thermally resistant surface for the fire.

What can go wrong?

The wood swells.
The inner mold could swell from the moisture in the concrete. If this happens, you may need to actually cut the wood to pry it free or just leave it in and let the fire slowly burn out.

Alternatives

Size this project up or down depending on your needs. You could add in a metal grate to use as a barbecue pit or build a cover and use it as an outdoor coffee table when not in use.

What if you don't want it anymore?

Break it apart with a sledgehammer and take the pieces to the concrete recycling center where it can have a new life in another project.

Lounge Chair

The ultimate in whiling away an afternoon is the lounge chair. It's a bit of a low rider, which makes it a little tough to get in, but once you do it's so comfortable that you won't want to get out. I made a pair of these for my parents' patio, and they are frequently put to good use for late-night chats around the fire pit.

Estimated Time:
6 hours

Estimated Cost:
Under $75

Materials:
1 12'-long 2×12
Template (available on HomeMade-Modern.com)
Craft or wood glue
2½" deck screws
4 6" L-brackets
⅜" × 1¼" × 32' trim board
1½" screws
Danish oil
Water sealant

Tools:
Ruler
Pencil
Circular saw
Clamps
Jigsaw
Cordless drill with driving bit
Belt sander
50- and 220-grit sandpaper
Clean rag
Paintbrush

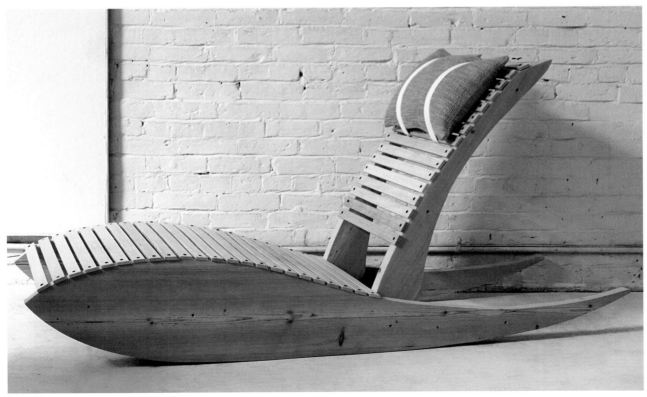

1: Cut the 12'-long 2×12 in half

You will need two pieces of 2×12 that are at least 6' to 10' long for this project. I recommend buying a single 12'-long 2×12 and having it cut at the store for you. Otherwise, measure, mark, and cut the 2×12 in half using the ruler, pencil, and circular saw.

2: Use the template to mark cuts

Print the template from HomeMade-Modern.com and glue it to one of the 6'-long 2×12s using the craft or wood glue. This template is a cutting guide, so make sure the edges are glued down and that it won't flap when you're cutting.

3: Cut the curves

Clamp the wood to your worktable. Use the jigsaw to make the curved cuts. Make sure that your blade is both sharp and designed for wood.

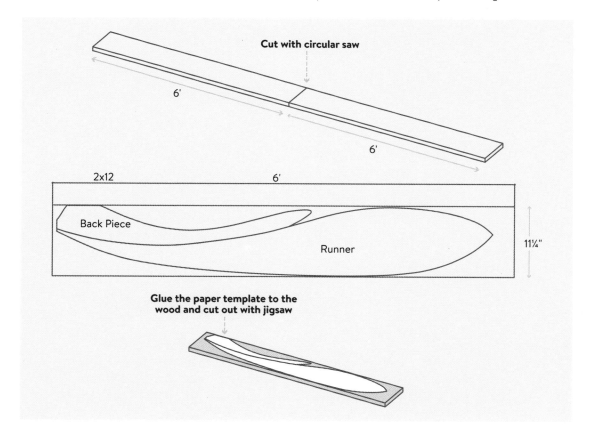

Cut with circular saw

6'

6'

2x12   6'

Back Piece

Runner

11¼"

Glue the paper template to the
wood and cut out with jigsaw

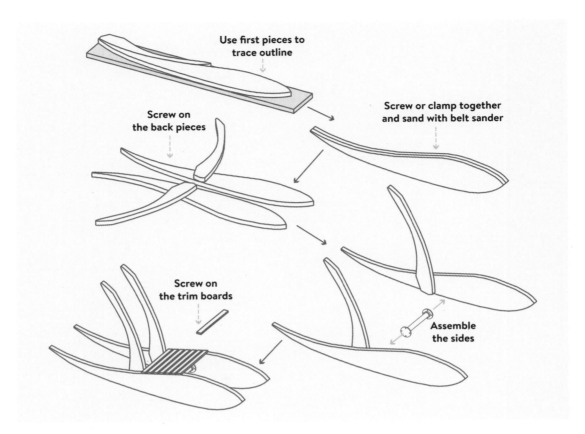

Use first pieces to trace outline

Screw on the back pieces

Screw or clamp together and sand with belt sander

Screw on the trim boards

Assemble the sides

4: Transfer the curve

Use the pieces you cut out in step 3 as the template for the remaining 6'-long 2×12. Place the cut pieces on top of the 6'-long 2×12 and trace around them using the pencil.

6: Screw the runners together

Using five or so 2½" deck screws, screw the pieces together using the cordless drill so that you can sand the edges of both at the same time.

5: Cut the second pieces

Clamp the wood to your worktable. Use the jigsaw to make the curved cuts. The more accurate you are with the cuts, the less time you'll have to spend sanding later.

7: Sand and shape the runners

This is the step that takes the most patience and time. Sand and shape the edges to make them identical to each other using the belt sander and 50-grit sandpaper. It's helpful to use a couple of L-brackets to secure the pieces to your work surface. Once the runners have identical profiles, repeat steps 6 and 7 for the two back pieces. Also use the orbital sander to sand off the glued-on template.

8: Screw on the back

Use the cordless drill and five 2½" deck screws to attach the back pieces to the runners. Cut some of the scrap pieces into braces that are 24" long and use L-brackets to connect the two runners. The ideal placement and angle of the back pieces depends on personal preference. Select a location and angle that works for you and make sure that both sides are the same.

9: Cut cross pieces

Cut the trim board into twenty-three 24"-long pieces for the seat and sixteen 21"-long pieces for the back.

10: Screw on the trim boards

Drive one 1½" screw on each end of the trim pieces into the runners. If the trim boards split, you'll need to pre-drill holes through them.

11: Stain and seal

Hand sand the wood with the 220-grit sandpaper. Remove the dust with the tack cloth. Use a cloth rag to rub a coat of Danish oil into the wood to finish the piece. If you want to use the piece outside, also apply a water sealant using the paintbrush.

What can go wrong?

Your jigsaw cuts are crooked.

When cutting curves on thick pieces of wood, the blade sometimes bends, resulting in an angled cut. A fresh, sharp blade and a properly adjusted jigsaw set to cut at 90 degrees helps prevent this. If your cuts are not perfect, don't worry; you'll be able to fix this during the sanding.

Alternatives

Use rope instead of trim boards. By drilling holes through the runners and stringing rope across, you can create a woven seat. If you try this technique I recommend using 24" pipes with flanges as spacers for the runners because they will be visible.

What if you don't want it anymore?

Disassemble the chair and use the wood for another project. The slats can be used to build wood storage crates.

Metric Conversion Chart

FROM	TO	MULTIPLY BY
Inches	Centimeters	2.54
Centimeters	Inches	0.4
Feet	Centimeters	30.5
Centimeters	Feet	0.03
Yards	Meters	0.9
Meters	Yards	1.1
Sq. Inches	Sq. Centimeters	6.45
Sq. Centimeters	Sq. Inches	0.16
Sq. Feet	Sq. Meters	0.09
Sq. Meters	Sq. Feet	10.8
Sq. Yards	Sq. Meters	0.8
Sq. Meters	Sq. Yards	1.2
Pounds	Kilograms	0.45
Kilograms	Pounds	2.2
Ounces	Grams	28.4
Grams	Ounces	0.035

ACKNOWLEDGMENTS

Thank you to the following individuals, who without their contributions and support, this book would not have been written:

My classmate who became my business partner, Stephanie Horowitz, for more than a decade of having my back.

Jamie and the ZED team for putting up with all the sawdust and noise.

Alice, for being the best creative Jane-of-All-Trades ever!

My siblings Jessie, Emily, and Nathan for creative input and leading inspiring lives.

Elle, for massive amounts of help and coffee knowledge.

All the wonderful people at Ryobi, but in particular, Stephanie Thomas and Brian Stearns.

The Quikrete Team, but in particular, Chad Corley.

My Profs. Milton Curry, Arthur Ovaska, and Pamela Zwehl-Burke.

Peggy Wang from BuzzFeed.

Friends and advisors who were always there with insight and encouragement: Nini, Ben, Tim, Dave, Jordan, Josh, Emile, Dan, Lisa, Shawn, Shuang, Caleb, Rod, Nicky, Al, and Will.

Special thanks to Billie and Fletcher!

The "author" isn't the only person who works directly on a book. I want to thank Amy Azzarito, Judy Linden, Jordana Tusman, and Frances Soo Ping Chow for all the help and patience.

And lastly, to all the viewers who supported my blog and inspired me by improving upon my creations.

INDEX

Page numbers in *italics* indicate photographs.

Notes